More Praise for *SuperTeams*

"Dr. Paul Marciano's latest book, *SuperTeams*, takes his bestselling concept of RESPECT one step further—TeamMe becomes TeamWe. Dr. Paul helps us better understand that teamwork is about relying on the strengths of each member through innovative cross-organizational ways. A must-read for anyone working collaboratively on a team or just trying to get along better with others."

> —*Gigi Schweikert, author of* Becoming a Team Player

"For the great leaders who value continuous learning, this is a magnificent book that teaches not only the 'what' of performance excellence in great leaders and teams, but also the 'why' and 'how' to achieve it. It is learning that takes great leaders to yet another level of performance excellence. As Paul and Clinton write: 'The RESPECT Model is an actionable philosophy—it is about acting in ways that actually demonstrate respect.' This is the stuff of greatness. Just as Jim Collins took us from Good to Great, Paul has done the same in taking us from individual to team."

> —*Michael M. Reuter, Director, Center for Leadership Development, Stillman School of Business, Seton Hall University*

"The authors have taken the innovative and people-focused RESPECT system and brilliantly applied it to the challenges of assembling, managing, and inspiring high-performing teams. Dr. Marciano's RESPECT framework lends itself very naturally to this detailed and thoughtful manual for evaluating and improving teams. Virtually every team and manager has something to learn from this impressive compilation of best practices and insightful recommendations."

> —*Krishnan Ramaswami, Partner, Vicente Capital*

"In my job, transforming a good team into a SuperTeam involves first exploring new things such as principles, knowledge, and behaviors and then entwining them in business and personal levels. *SuperTeams* altered my perspective in both areas. To me it's not just a great book. It's the absolute manual to exceeding my clients' expectations in team engagement and bottom-line results."

> —*Yiannis Koutsoumaris, Managing Partner and Behavioral Master Coach, inwards*

"The book introduces a new-age strategy for development of commonsense values across corporate cultures. It is a great book about the anatomy of pure human respect, a base-stone of corporate values and sustainable team results. I appreciate the ability of the authors to develop a number of simple, practical, and ready-to-use tools. I was able to use them right away in my team. SuperTeams is also a new challenge for HR: developing teams with large added value to the company."

—*Dr. Kiril Ribarov, Head of Training and Development Department, CEZ Group*

"At the end of the day it is teams, whether tightly or loosely coupled, that drive business success. Extending the RESPECT Model to teams in many ways completes the toolkit leaders need to fully engage their workforce and help their organizations thrive. I've found the explanations and discussions in *SuperTeams* straightforward, practical, and extremely relevant to the challenges of the modern workplace. I would encourage all leaders to embrace the lessons and principles explained here to create powerful workplaces with exceptional performance."

—*William F. Hills, Senior Vice President, Information Services, Navy Federal Credit Union*

"Paul and Clinton provide a road map we can all use when constructing teams in our organizations. The fundamental principle of success is built around *respect*! Without that foundation, I am not sure success is achievable."

—*Peggy McGrane, HR Director, Marsh & McLennan Agency LLC*

"Marciano and Wingrove bring proven strategies to life with real-world examples drawn from experiences working with successful teams. This book provides an excellent training model that organizations can both appreciate and easily implement to engage their teams in becoming SuperTeams!"

—*Diane Piraino-Koury, McDonald's Owner/Operator*

"Dr. Paul Marciano has done it again. Not only does he make the case for how lack of respect is at the heart of most of our toughest leadership and teamwork problems, but he offers practical, easy-to-implement steps to improve in both areas. I highly recommend this book."

—*Jack Nestor, HR Director, DPT Laboratories*

"Move over 'forming, storming, norming, and performing,' there's a new approach to team performance called RESPECT. Marciano and Wingrove provide a fresh new model that all leaders can use to turn average teams into SuperTeams."

—*Kevin Kruse,* New York Times *bestselling author of* We

"Practical and valuable. Paul and Clinton provide methods to help create, motivate, and sustain SuperTeams that consistently deliver and exceed customer expectations. I was able to apply the learnings right away and see the difference in the performance of my teams."

—*Michelle Mosolgo, Executive Director Enterprise Programs, Merck*

"This book conveys the extraordinary power of the RESPECT Model of team development. The book confirms something that Caliper has found through years of research: that when people are treated with respect, they work harder and truly create SuperTeams. *SuperTeams* should be read by everyone involved in creating or building teams."

—*Herb Greenberg, PhD, CEO and Founder, Caliper*

"Leadership is the absolute key to business success. Leaders form strategy and create strong and committed teams of talented and motivated people that produce extraordinary business success. Paul and Clinton have covered this critical aspect eloquently in their book—ignore it at your peril!"

—*Roger Phillips, former CEO, Iveco Ford Ltd.*

"*SuperTeams* makes clear two important and interconnected ideas—that the success of teams in all kinds of organizations is dependent on the relationships among team members and that all team members play a crucial role building and maintaining those relationships. Full of practical advice and interactive exercises, *SuperTeams* is a resource that leaders, managers, and team members can return to time and again as they strive to create and maintain the context for success."

—*Jim Dlugos, President, Saint Joseph's College of Maine*

"Marciano and Wingrove provide an indispensable guide for all team members and leaders seeking to create a SuperTeam and exceed their customers' expectations."

—*Beverly Kaye, coauthor of* Love 'Em or Lose 'Em

"Running a company of any size requires knowing how to manage people effectively. Without exception, my colleagues and I prefer leadership to management—although managing has its place. But I want to be a great leader, and *SuperTeams* reinvigorates me to do those important activities to bring out the best in my teams. *SuperTeams* teaches me to return to important leadership activities such as sharing my long-term vision consistently—all the way through living the values and behaviors by which my organization will thrive. In my opinion, this is a great book for every business leader. However, this is required reading for small businesses who want tremendous tools to help them unleash their team's performance."

—*Daniel J. Rehal, President, Vision2Voice*

SuperTeams

SuperTeams

Using the
PRINCIPLES OF
RESPECT™
to Unleash Explosive
Business Performance

Paul L. Marciano, PhD
Clinton Wingrove

New York   Chicago   San Francisco   Athens   London   Madrid
Mexico City   Milan   New Delhi   Singapore   Sydney   Toronto

Except as permitted under the United States Copyright Act of 1976, no part of this publication may be reproduced or distributed in any form or by any means, or stored in a database or retrieval system, without the prior written permission of the publisher.

1 2 3 4 5 6 7 8 9 0   DOC/DOC   1 2 0 9 8 7 6 5 4

ISBN   978-0-07-183042-3
MHID   0-07-183042-1

e-ISBN 978-0-07-182938-0
e-MHID 0-07-182938-5

RESPECT is a trademark of Whiteboard, LLC.

McGraw-Hill Education books are available at special quantity discounts to use as premiums and sales promotions or for use in corporate training programs. To contact a representative, please visit the Contact Us pages at www.mhprofessional.com.

To the best team members we could ever ask for,
our beautiful wives, Karen and Carole

Contents

Introduction

by Dr. Paul Marciano

My wife, Karen, is an elementary school teacher, and she once asked me to read the children's book *Madeline* to her second-grade class. (My maternal grandfather, Ludwig Bemelmans, is the author and illustrator.) As soon as you walk into Karen's classroom, you see a poster with the words "Respect, Resourcefulness, and Responsibility"—the three Rs by which she runs her classroom. After I finished reading, a small boy, Dhananjay, raised his hand and asked, "Are you a teacher?" At first I replied, "No," but then I changed my answer and said, "Actually, I am a teacher. I teach adults about respect." He responded, "Why, do they forget?" Out of the mouths of babes.

I am passionate about spreading respect in the workplace for two reasons. First, people fundamentally deserve to be treated with respect—it is simply the right thing to do. Second, doing so has a profound effect on a team's effectiveness and an organization's bottom line. Why? Because when team members feel respected, they become engaged with their work and with one another, which leads to increased initiative, productivity, creativity, customer satisfaction, compliance, loyalty, employee wellness, and retention. When we feel respected we become more committed, and we are willing to give more of ourselves than is required. When we feel disrespected, we disengage. By the way, this holds just as true for our personal relationships.

Relationships—personal and professional—work only within the context of respect.

When *Carrots and Sticks Don't Work: Build a Culture of Employee Engagement with the Principles of RESPECT™* was published in 2010, I could have hardly imagined the response. I have received e-mails from hundreds of people around the globe expressing their gratitude and affirming the critical role that respect plays in the workplace. Regardless of culture, respect resonates with us as human beings. Of the many e-mails I received, few stand out as much as the following from Mostafa Radmard—a human resources professional in Tehran, Iran:

> *The RESPECT Model is not only beneficial for engaging different levels of employees, from simple workers to top managers. . . . Its principles go beyond national cultures. Our experiences, like the author's, confirm that what makes Iranian employees motivated, even in tough financial conditions, is the feeling of respect. The RESPECT Model could be prescribed as a cure for the ill management attitudes and practices in Iran.*

Respect matters, and it matters regardless of nationality, race, gender, or age. Obviously, how respect is defined and demonstrated differs greatly by various demographic variables. And you don't have to compare nations to find wide variations. For example, in most small rural towns in America, it would be considered quite rude to walk past someone without saying, "Hello." In contrast, such behavior would be considered socially odd in most large cities. I can't remember a time that I walked down the streets of New York City and had a total stranger sincerely ask me how my day was going.

Why This Book?

I would like to think that the level of respect in the workplace has increased since the publication of *Carrots and Sticks Don't Work.*

Sadly, surveys generally show that worker morale and engagement are at an all-time low while stress is at an all-time high. Perhaps most shocking are the staggeringly high rates of bullying that people report witnessing and experiencing. In fact, the situation is nothing short of an epidemic. What is most disturbing is that in some organizations, bullies actually thrive. The most obvious cases exist within sales-oriented organizations in which those who bring in the "big bucks" are viewed as indispensable and allowed to act with impunity.

Clinton and I have worked with many organizations in which individuals regularly belittle, undermine, threaten, and yell at their coworkers without any consequences—even after multiple complaints to human resources. In the words of one frustrated human resources manager, "I'm going to be the best witness the prosecution has." The CEO's position: "We can't afford to lose him." **You can't afford to keep him!**

Beyond the obvious reasons that bullying is "wrong," such behavior constitutes harassment, and it contributes to a hostile workplace environment and can form the basis for a lawsuit. In fact, other countries—most prominently Australia—have established clear anti-bullying laws, and, as of the writing of this book, more than 20 states in the United States are considering such laws. Without question, those bullied will bring lawsuits against their organizations, and many will win. We have **never** seen an instance where a bully was fired and there was any significant loss in productivity or profitability. In fact, just the opposite is most often the case.

Many organizations claim "respect" as a core value. For most, however, the concept exists more on paper than in practice. In conducting research for this book, I had the pleasure of interviewing Edward Deustch, founder and managing partner of the prestigious law firm McElroy, Deutsch, Mulvaney & Carpenter, LLP.

Over the past 30 years Ed has guided his organization based on the principle of respect and what he calls the "No Jerk Rule." There is a very clear expectation that everyone will treat one another, from senior partner to newest mailroom clerk, with respect regardless of position or tenure. And Ed won't hesitate to let people go when they act like a *jerk* irrespective of the potential loss in revenue they may represent. Firing someone for acting disrespectfully toward a colleague is both the "right" thing to do and best for the business.

In Ed's words, "When we have parted ways with lawyers who did not have the necessary respect for others, it greatly enhanced morale and loyalty, and it led to greater productivity and profits every single time." A lot more organizations would be a whole lot more successful if they had Ed at the helm.

What Is *SuperTeams* About?

SuperTeams is a book about the importance of respect in the workplace and the critical role that it plays in creating highly engaged and satisfied team members who in turn create high-functioning teams who consistently exceed expectations. The intention of this book is to empower team members and team leaders to take action to enhance the functioning and success of their team. Like *Carrots and Sticks Don't Work*, this book is based on the RESPECT Model, and it provides readers with specific, pragmatic, and tangible strategies and techniques to foster a culture of respect and increase team member engagement, productivity, and satisfaction.

Please note, this book was written to serve both as a follow-up to *Carrots and Sticks Don't Work* and, at the same time, to stand on its own. Toward that end, some key concepts that appear in *Carrots and Sticks Don't Work* will be reviewed here in an abbreviated form. In all cases, we have provided fresh examples and presented the material with a focus on teams.

Who Will Benefit from This Book?

This book was written as much for individual team members as for supervisors, managers, and human resources professionals. We take the position that individual team members are as responsible for their own engagement and their teams' functioning as is their team leader. Thus, this book will serve as a resource for anyone in your organization who belongs to a team.

What Will You Get out of This Book?

Readers can expect to learn the following:

1. What constitutes a SuperTeam and how your team measures up
2. The power of respect in our personal and professional lives
3. The relationship between respect and engagement
4. The RESPECT Team Model and how each of its seven drivers contributes to the creation of a SuperTeam
5. Various team configurations and the implications for maximizing team effectiveness
6. How to identify high-potential team members
7. How to deal with team member entry and exit
8. SuperTeam Rules
9. How to appropriately reward and recognize teams and team members for their accomplishments
10. How to deal powerfully with diversity issues on teams

How Will You Get the Most Value out of This Book?

The book is filled with thought questions, mini-quizzes, and exercises to help you put its concepts and strategies on the playing field of your life—both professionally and personally. *SuperTeams* is not meant to be a philosophical treatise on how to deal with hypothetical situations; it is intended to be used as a hands-on resource to make a difference for you and the teams on which you currently participate and, ultimately, to make yours a SuperTeam.

Bonus Material

Readers are invited to visit the website www.SuperTeamsTheBook. com for bonus material and additional resources, including answers to SuperTough Issues such as how to deal with a team leader or team members you don't respect, what to do when you don't feel respected by your team leader or team members, and how to increase your own level of engagement. You'll also find various worksheets to help you in your quest to create a SuperTeam, as well as a list of our favorite team quotes. And you are welcome to contact us directly at Paul@PaulMarciano.com and Clinton@ClintonWingrove.com.

Our Team

Writing a book is a journey, and like any journey, it is made better by the company you keep. When I was presented with the opportunity to write *SuperTeams*, I decided that this project would be best served by actually making it a team effort. I am extremely grateful and honored to be joined by Clinton Wingrove—a man for whom I have much personal and professional respect. One of the most passionate and hard-working people I know, Clinton brings a wealth of real-world experience and expertise, having formed and managed teams, and having consulted with organizations around the globe. His wisdom and insights on individual and team performance and how their potential can be realized have resulted in a far stronger and more valuable book than I could have created on my own.

Clinton and I have been blessed with a wonderful team leader—our editor Casie Vogel. She has been a steadfast proponent of this work from start to finish, and she has provided us with support and expert guidance throughout. We appreciate her giving us the independence to stray at times and appreciate even more her shepherding us back to the path when we wandered too far. And we have our wonderful wives, Karen and Carole, without whose endless encouragement, support, and patience our team could not have researched and written this book. Last but not least, we so greatly appreciate those organizations that generously participated in our research for this book and would like to specifically acknowledge The Earle Companies, DFAS, Unimasters, and Family Fare C Stores. The creation of *SuperTeams* has truly been a collaborative effort and a wonderful experience. Having great team members makes all the difference to the quality of the work and the journey.

Thank You

Thank you for your interest in our work and for helping to spread respect in the workplace—and the world. *Namaste.*

SuperTeams

PART I

What Is a SuperTeam?

The strength of the team is each individual member.
The strength of each member is the team.
—Phil Jackson, Coach, Chicago Bulls

Overview

In this brief part opener we define the concept of a SuperTeam and ask you to think about how your team measures up. Begin to think about what would be possible if your team achieved SuperTeam status. We hope that the chapters that follow will help you do just that.

What Is a Team?

A team is generally defined as two or more people working together to achieve a common goal. Traditional teams are characterized by a leader, clear goals, individual roles, specific processes and practices, and a means of intra-team communication. Teams have their own culture and social mores. They are traditionally stable in team member composition, and they exist in perpetuity. Team members tend to have little autonomy or decision-making authority—their team leader makes the decisions, sets the priorities, and manages the workflow. The fundamental assumption is that teams are created because they can produce a higher-quality deliverable more effectively and efficiently than individuals working alone can. As we will discuss in later chapters, this is not always true.

What Is a SuperTeam?

As tempted as we are to engage in a deep philosophical discussion on exactly how to define a SuperTeam, we offer the following instead:

A SuperTeam is a team that consistently delivers superior performance relative to customer expectations.

These expectations typically relate to quality, efficiency, and cost. It is critical to remain focused on the customers' evaluation of team effectiveness rather than focusing on success as defined by team members, team leaders, or team sponsors—each of which can differ dramatically.

Consider, for example, the primary team involved in the creation and publication of this book: Clinton, Paul, and our wonderful editor Casie who represents the larger team at McGraw-Hill. Success for team McGraw-Hill is defined by the number of books sold. In contrast, Paul might define success as getting a higher number of keynote speaking requests, while Clinton might define winning as getting increased consulting opportunities or software sales. In a more typical business unit, one person might win if he gets the opportunity to work with more high-profile clients, while another sees winning as getting more autonomy and decision-making responsibility. Perhaps someone else hopes for a promotion while another defines success by the size of her bonus, and another by his work-life balance.

While there is nothing intrinsically wrong with individuals or teams having distinct goals, doing so lends itself to a misalignment of efforts and reduced collaboration as people pursue their personal agendas. In fact, unfortunately, there are times when team members' goals are actually in direct opposition and those who should be collaborators turn into competitors.

The extent to which any team member achieves her personal goals is irrelevant to achieving SuperTeam status, which is defined entirely by customer satisfaction. Thus, the true measure of whether our team qualifies as a SuperTeam depends wholly on whether our product—this book—exceeds your expectations. We certainly hope it does.

Wrap-Up

As you will see, achieving SuperTeam status is no small feat, and, quite frankly, it may be unrealistic for many teams. Would you consider yours a SuperTeam? Does your team consistently exceed customer expectations? Does your team have the potential to become a SuperTeam? What would that take? Obviously, we don't know your team, but we do know that becoming a SuperTeam starts with you. Throughout this book, we will beat on the following drum: What can you do to make a difference on your team?

Taking liberty with Paul's favorite quote—*Be the change you want to see in the world* by Mahatma Gandhi:

Be the change you want to see in your team.

Up Next

SuperTeams are composed of highly engaged team members who willingly, and of their own volition, go above and beyond. In the following chapter we will take on the topics of what employee engagement actually is, how engaged you and your team are, and how to increase engagement.

CHAPTER 1

Engagement

Individual commitment to a group effort—that is
what makes a team work, a company work, a society
work, a civilization work.

—*Vince Lombardi, Coach, Green Bay Packers*

Overview

The issue of employee engagement and its importance to organizational effectiveness has received considerable attention over the past two decades. Despite the volume of research and writing that has been done on this fairly simple concept, there continues to be considerable confusion, particularly when it comes to distinguishing it from motivation.

In this chapter, you will learn:

- The definition of engagement and how it differs from motivation
- Characteristic behaviors of highly engaged employees
- The role engagement plays in SuperTeams
- Different targets of engagement
- Your level of engagement and that of your team members
- The differences between TeamMe and TeamWe players
- Strategies to increase team engagement

As a starting point, take a moment to reflect on the following questions.

SUPERSTARTER QUESTIONS

1. Think about the job in which you were the least engaged and the one in which you were the most engaged. How did engagement impact your willingness to go above and beyond in each job?
2. How engaged are you in your current job?
3. How can you tell the difference between an engaged versus a disengaged team member?
4. What causes some team members to be engaged and others not to be so?
5. What causes engaged employees to become disengaged?

ENGAGEMENT SELF-ASSESSMENT

Instructions: Read each statement below, and, using the following scale, decide how accurately it describes you:

Strongly disagree: 0 points
Disagree: 1 point
Agree: 2 points
Strongly agree: 3 points

Place the point value of your answer choice on the blank line at the beginning of each of the following statements:

_____ 1. **You take the initiative to learn new skills.**
_____ 2. **You contribute above and beyond what is expected.**
_____ 3. **You jump in and help team members when they are struggling with their work.**
_____ 4. **You take pride in your work.**
_____ 5. **You make improvement suggestions to your team members and team leader.**

_____ **Total score**

INTERPRETING YOUR SCORES

0 to 5: Going to work is a painful experience. You don't feel good about the work you do or people with whom you work. Workdays are long and likely tedious. You are simply "punching a clock" and doing only what is required of you. You feel unappreciated and likely disrespected by your teammates and/or the team leader. If you're smart, instead of complaining and feeling like a victim, you're spending your time and energy looking for a new job opportunity.

6 to 10: Like most people, you have your good days and bad days. Your level of motivation, engagement, and satisfaction depends on the project or people with whom you are working, as well as the extent to which you are recognized appropriately for your contributions. Focus on what you like about your job and what you get out of it personally. The more engaged you are, the more productive you will be, and the more satisfied you will be with your job. What can you do to become more engaged with your work and team members?

11 to 15: Especially as you approach the top score, you actually look forward to going to work. You feel good about the work that you do and are appropriately recognized for your accomplishments by your team members and team leader. You have opportunities to learn and grow which keeps you stimulated. There is a mutual level of respect with your team members and leader. You are a true team player; others can count on you to do your job at an extremely high level and can also count on your support.

ASSESSMENT REFLECTION EXERCISE

Unfortunately, most people do not feel fully engaged in their work. In fact, many feel quite disengaged. Please take a moment to consider the factors that cause people—especially you—to engage and disengage from their work and coworkers. Also, if you are currently disengaged, what are some strategies to put yourself fully back in the game? (You may find suggestions on how to do just this by visiting the section "SuperTough Issues" on our website: www.SuperTeamsTheBook.com.)

What Is Employee Engagement?

If you're reading this book, there is a good chance that you're highly familiar with the concept of employee engagement. At the most basic level, *engagement* refers to an individual's commitment and willingness to do what it takes to get the job done. Highly engaged team members choose to apply their talents, energy, and care toward their work, and they exhibit the following behaviors:

- They exert high levels of discretionary effort—that is, they go above and beyond.
- They are willing (or even desire) to remain on their team through periods of change and adversity. Engaged employees are "hardy," and they don't get derailed when the going gets tough.
- They take initiative, and they are proactive, including taking responsibility for their own development.
- They hold themselves accountable for delivering on their promises.
- They work collaboratively and synergistically with other team members.

Given these qualities, it is not surprising that research has demonstrated the positive impact of employee engagement on an organization's bottom line through increased profitability, productivity, efficiency, quality, creativity, safety, compliance, employee well-being, and retention.

TeamMe Players

Sometimes, individual players have the greatest level of commitment to themselves. TeamMe players have a decidedly negative impact on team functioning as other team members become resentful of their selfish behavior. Team members may also come to resent and lose respect for the team leader who allows such behavior to continue. Unfortunately, we find TeamMe players all too prevalent. A TeamMe attitude is typically personality driven, and it is extremely difficult to change. Attempts by team members and the team leader to bring such individuals back into the fold typically have a limited and short-lived impact. Screening out TeamMe players before they get on your team is critical. We will discuss how to identify and recruit TeamWe players later in the book.

We see TeamMe examples frequently in professional sports where most players have no allegiance to the organization, team members, or fans, and they switch teams based on who offers the most lucrative contract. We see such behavior in our workplaces, especially among those in younger generations who rarely stay with organizations more than a few years and often leave with little or no notice. Of course, there has been a profound decline in the loyalty that organizations demonstrate toward their employees. In many companies, there is a feeling that no one's job is safe. This cultural shift away from team loyalty, and the subsequent revolving door of team members, has had significant implications for team functioning.

TeamWe Players

In stark contrast to TeamMe players are those who are highly engaged with not just their work but also their other team members' work. One of the most fundamental characteristics of highly engaged team members is not only that they take responsibility for themselves but that they take responsibility for one another. They have one another's backs. Military, fire, and police units depend on this level of commitment to one another to survive. In organizations, having one another's backs can take many forms, including not letting those outside the team—or inside—speak derogatively about other team members, helping team members with their workload, and giving one another straight feedback. Critically, such team members watch out for one another's safety. Like the issue of respect, most organizations profess a strong commitment to safety. Unfortunately, both concepts exist more in the organizations' philosophies than in their practices.

The vast majority of injuries and deaths that occur on the job are preventable. In the construction and manufacturing industries, the most basic rule of equipment repair or maintenance is called Lock Out

Tag Out (LOTO). Put simply, this is the practice of locking a machine such that it cannot be accidentally turned on. Every team member is aware of this core safety practice. Yet, time and again employees are injured or killed because this procedure is ignored and, critically for this conversation, with multiple team members watching. Such an incident would simply never occur on a SuperTeam because TeamWe players would step forward and yell, "STOP!" Would yours?

According to safety and organizational change expert Phil LaDuke:

> The most common reason for LOTO violations isn't willful disregard for safety or recklessness, it's simple human error—the person responsible for locking out screws up, forgets, or believes the procedure isn't necessary in that circumstance. Companies struggle with creating a brother's keeper mentality for a variety of reasons. In many union shops this could be seen as "duplicate supervision," a concept that holds that a person has one, and only one, supervisor. In other cases, people are reluctant to confront the situation for fear of an aggressive response, but in most cases that I have seen, the reluctance is—plainly and simply—a reluctance to embarrass the offending worker. Some people believe working unsafe is their right. I would say that a TeamWe member cares about his or her safety because of the ramifications of any injury for the team. The burden of preventing these accidents (which by the way are disproportionately fatal) falls not on the person doing the job but on those AROUND the person doing the job.

TEAM ENGAGEMENT ASSESSMENT

Instructions: Read each statement below, and, using the following scale, decide how accurately it describes your team members:

Strongly disagree: 0 points
Disagree: 1 point
Agree: 2 points
Strongly agree: 3 points

Place the point value of your answer choice on the blank line at the beginning of each of the following statements:

_____ 1. **Your team members deliver on their promises and commitments.**

_____ 2. **They contribute above and beyond what is expected of them.**

_____ 3. **They jump in and help one another out with their work.**

_____ 4. **They take pride in being part of the team.**

_____ 5. **They put the interests of the team above their own.**

_____   **Total score**

INTERPRETING YOUR SCORES

0 to 5: Yours is a highly dysfunctional team, but then you knew that. Team members, including most likely your team leader, look out only for themselves and their own best interests. People watch out for their own backs—as they should in this environment. Scores in this range describe a TeamMe culture. Quite frankly, it is nearly impossible to change such a culture, and we encourage you to be on the lookout for other opportunities.

6 to 10: Either the majority of team members have an average level of engagement to one another, or some are quite engaged while others are disengaged. In the first case, the team is usually quite large and/or team members work independently and may even be located in different offices. It is difficult for people to feel committed to one another when they have quite limited physical interaction. Team members need to take the time to get to know one another on a more personal level. Bimodal distributions of engagement are often a sign that cliques exist. In such situations, some team members may feel ostracized, and they may also feel that their work is not valued. This situation is most easily improved by the engaged team members taking the initiative to reach out and get to know their less engaged colleagues and letting them know how much their efforts are appreciated.

11 to 15: It feels good to be on your team where people care about one another and the work that they do. People keep their promises and commitments, and they deliver high-quality work. Team members actively support and collaborate with one another. Personal agendas come in a distant second to the mission of the team and the goal of exceeding your customers' expectations. Yours has the makings of a SuperTeam!

ASSESSMENT REFLECTION EXERCISE

Rarely are all team members fully engaged. Identify a team member whose engagement has waned over time. Express your genuine concern. For example: "Tom, I'm concerned about you. I've noticed that over the past few weeks you've fallen behind in your work and participate a lot less in our team meetings. You also just don't seem as upbeat as you usually are. Is there something going on that you would like to talk about?" Of course, if you believe that there is a specific incident that triggered the change in behavior, you can reference it. For example: "Ever since the boss gave Nancy that account, you've seemed a lot less engaged."

Your goal is to have your team members open up and express any upsets or concerns, so that you can then look for ways that you can help by offering a different perspective or advice. Just showing that you care and allowing the team members to vent their feelings may be extremely helpful. We know that things will not get better if the individuals keep their concerns to themselves.

SuperStars

SuperTeams are composed entirely of highly engaged team members; however, that doesn't mean that they are composed entirely of SuperStars. The word *superstars* suggests individuals who stand out from their peers in terms of their talents, efforts, and contributions. SuperStars are also more likely to be TeamMe players, and, even if they are not, they may be viewed as such by other team members who tend to become resentful of the attention and accolades directed toward those individuals. Of course, SuperStars who do play for TeamMe take every opportunity to shine the spotlight on their own accomplishments.

> Anybody that has their own agenda that's separate from the team's
> won't be around long.
>
> —*Bill Parcells, Coach, New York Giants*

In truth, some team members are more talented and will contribute more than others. However, on a SuperTeam such individuals consistently direct the attention away from themselves and towards the entire team and its accomplishments. Such individuals also typically help to coach, mentor, and inspire less skilled and experienced team members. Most important, they serve as role models when it comes to work ethic, commitment, and dedication. A SuperTeam might have one, none, or many SuperStars—the number doesn't matter. All that matters is that the team is composed of highly engaged and hard-working TeamWe players whose main objective is to contribute as much as they can to help the team win.

Multiple Targets of Engagement

Engagement is nearly always defined in terms of the relationship between individuals and their commitment to their work. However, as we've just discussed, engagement also exists between individuals and their fellow team members. In addition, individuals have some level of engagement with their team leader, their customers, and the broader organization. In the context of these relationships, engagement continues to be defined by the extent to which people are dedicated, loyal, and committed. It is common that people feel more engaged with one target than another. For example, nurses might feel highly dedicated to their patients and not at all committed to their direct supervisors.

Unfortunately, it is nearly impossible to achieve SuperTeam status without team members being highly engaged with all of the targets.

Engagement Versus Motivation

As discussed in detail in Paul's book *Carrots and Sticks Don't Work*, organizations continue to use the terms *engagement* and *motivation* interchangeably despite the fact that there are significant and meaningful differences between the two. Motivated team members are not necessarily engaged. Dangle a large enough "carrot" and people will jump as high as they can, but it doesn't mean that they care why they are jumping. Critically, if they don't win, they are less likely to give discretionary effort going forward—even if there is a dangling carrot. Billions of dollars are spent annually by companies trying to motivate—"bribe"—employees into working harder. Forty years of research demonstrates that traditional reward and recognition programs intended to motivate employees are ineffective. In fact, they actually lead to an overall decrease in staff morale and productivity. Moreover, such programs detract from the pride individuals take in their work—and pride is a core characteristic of any SuperTeam member.

Why Is Team Engagement So Challenging?

Research suggests that only a fraction of employees are highly engaged. Obviously, this is one reason that so few SuperTeams exist. Many factors contribute to team dysfunction, including different personalities, backgrounds, and agendas; poor communication; incompetent leadership; a lack of resources and skilled team members; and a history of interpersonal conflict. One of the biggest killers of team engagement is the lack of personal connection that team members often feel with one another.

Building a team is about building relationships.

People are only able to "relate" to one another once they have connected on a personal level. It is virtually impossible for people who don't know one another to feel committed to one another. Get to know your team members.

I Don't Know Your Name

It never ceases to amaze us how coworkers who often spend more time with one another than they do with their families know so little about each other. In fact, it is not uncommon in larger teams for people not to even know each other's names! Paul once conducted a RESPECT team building workshop for an organization with a total of 150 employees. During a "get to know you" icebreaker exercise, a woman raised her hand and pointed to a lady at another table and said, "I've been working here for eight years, and I've been passing you in the hallway for eight years, and I am embarrassed to say that I don't know your name." A lot of people in the room didn't know either of their names.

Are there people you have been passing for years whose names you still don't know? The next time you see one of these people, try this: "I know that we've both been here a long time, and this is very awkward, but I don't know [or remember] your name." A little authenticity goes a long way in this world.

SuperTips for Getting Connected

Teamwork depends on team members feeling connected to one another—and in SuperTeams, the team members feel extremely connected to one another. There is no more effective way for people to become connected than by simply getting to know one another on a personal level. (Obviously, individuals and cultures differ on what they consider to be appropriate social boundaries. One should always err on the side of being less intrusive.) There are many ways for team members to become better acquainted. Simple and low-cost pizza parties and ice cream socials provide such opportunities; of course, these events aren't particularly effective as people tend to talk to only those they already know.

One organization with which we worked had a designated table in the cafeteria where a different person from each department sat and had lunch each day. Typically no one knew anyone else. The CEO always made it a point to have lunch at the table at least once a month. Obviously, an easy way to connect with someone on your team is simply to invite that person out to lunch.

Start with the person you know least, or better yet, the person with whom you may have the most conflict. As new team members join, make sure that they spend some one-to-one time with all the other team members for the sole purpose of getting to know them.

Our favorite example comes from a large accounting firm where the team leader, Sam, managed a staff of more than 50 data entry personnel. Many of these people had worked "together" for years without really knowing one another. It was the kind of place where people barely acknowledged one another's existence walking down the hallways. Sam decided that he wanted to do something to improve this situation and hopefully the morale of the staff that had been quite low due to budget cuts.

There was a large bare wall that most people passed by on the way to their cubicles. He decided to cover it with corkboard and divide it into three sections. Every month three team members were chosen at random to decorate a portion of the corkboard with whatever they liked. They were encouraged to attach personal items that would let other team members get to know them. People posted lots of pictures of their families, pets, and friends. There was a lot of sports memorabilia displayed that led to friendships and friendly rivalries. Some people posted their favorite quotes, pictures from a recent vacation, and even their bucket list. Our favorite: a woman who posted her newly signed divorce papers! (Quite a clever way to advertise that you're available!) Although people were not forced to participate, nearly everyone did, and it profoundly changed team morale and the extent to which people felt connected to one another, and, other than the corkboard, it cost nothing. What creative activities can your team come up with to strengthen connections?

On Your Playing Field

The more team members are engaged with one another, the more collaboration that occurs and, thus, the more effective the team. As always, start with what *you* can do. Identify the team members whom you know least well, and invite them out for lunch. Use the time to find out more about them on a personal level. For example, you might ask about their significant other, children, pets, where they grew up, the college they attended, their hobbies, or where they like to vacation. The questions don't matter as much as the intent to connect with your team members at this more personal level. Whom do you choose?

Wrap-Up

No team ever achieved great things without players who were fully invested in the game and with one another. Individual team members must assume responsibility for their own engagement with their work, coworkers, team leaders, and customers. Are you fully engaged? If not, what are you going to do about it? Being a SuperTeam starts with you!

Up Next

In the following chapter we will take on the issue of respect and learn why people are willing to die for it. We will also discuss the relationship between respect and power, and we will challenge the most highly regarded model of human motivation.

CHAPTER 2 # Dying for Respect

I'm not concerned with your liking or disliking me.
All I ask is that you **respect** me as a human being.
—*Jackie Robinson*

Overview

We've met many people who have said that they don't care about being liked, but seldom anyone who claimed that he or she was indifferent when it comes to being respected. While most people, of course, would prefer to be liked and respected, when push comes to shove, most choose respect.

In this brief chapter, you will learn:

- Why human beings care so much about being respected
- The relationship between respect and survival
- Our argument to revise Maslow's Hierarchy of Needs model
- The relationship between respect and being a powerful leader

As a starting point, take a moment to reflect on the following questions.

SUPERSTARTER QUESTIONS

1. Is it more important to you to be liked or respected? Why?
2. Do you think that there are generational differences when it comes to the issue of respect? If so, what are they?
3. Should people in authority automatically be given respect due to their position?
4. Do you respect your manager? Why or why not?
5. Why do you think that respect is a matter of survival?

When You Are Respected, You Are Protected

Respect is a matter of survival. Since human beings first began living in tribes, the most respected members of a community were the most "protected" because they were viewed as valuable to their tribe. (Or they were respected and protected because they were in positions of authority.) Such individuals also tended to have access to the best food and shelter and to the strongest reproductive partners. Respect has played a central role in all societies and world religions. Maintaining social order depends on citizens respecting their rulers, laws, and gods. If a subject disrespected the king, he could lose his head.

The relationship between disrespect and death may be more significant than you think. Defeated Japanese samurai committed ritual suicide (*hara-kiri*) in order to restore their honor. The Hatfield-McCoy feud was largely fueled by the desire to maintain family honor. Gang members kill one another entirely over the issue of respect—protecting one's turf, colors, and honor. If you allow yourself to be disrespected, it makes you appear weak and vulnerable.

Duels, also known as "affairs of honor," were common from the Middle Ages through the nineteenth century. Men were willing to kill or risk being killed to defend their honor or that of a lady. One of the most famed duels occurred between Aaron Burr, the sitting American vice president, and Alexander Hamilton, the former secretary of the Treasury. During the 1804 New York gubernatorial race, Hamilton publicly and severely attacked Burr's character; in order to restore his reputation, Burr challenged Hamilton to a duel during which Burr killed him. Although dueling may be out of vogue, defending one's honor and reputation is still very much alive.

Maslow Revisited

Abraham Maslow developed arguably the most well-known and widely accepted theory of motivation known as the Hierarchy of Needs. In his model, Maslow proposed five levels of human needs:

1. **Physiological needs.** Food, water, air, sex, sleep, homeostasis, and excretion
2. **Safety.** Security of body, employment, resources, morality, the family, health, and property
3. **Love and belonging.** Friendship, family belonging, and sexual intimacy
4. **Esteem.** Self-esteem, confidence, achievement, respect of others, and respect by others
5. **Self-actualization.** Morality, creativity, spontaneity, ability to solve problems, lack of prejudice, and acceptance of facts

Maslow maintained that individuals had to satisfy lower-level needs before they were motivated to pursue those at the next level. For example, pursuing friendships would matter only after safety needs had been met, and safety needs were pursued only after the most basic of physiological needs were met. Water and air trump friends every time.

Without question, Maslow's model has stood the test of time. With great respect, however, we would like to challenge the placement of "respect by others" on the hierarchy. We contend—and hope you agree—that respect *is* a matter of survival. Thus, we suggest that "respect by others" actually belongs two levels down as part of the need for Safety. (Our esteem of others, however, we believe appropriately remains on the Esteem level.) We do not believe that such an argument has ever been made and would welcome your opinions on this matter.

Respect = Power

Another reason human beings care so much about respect is its relationship with power, where power is defined as the ability to influence others. We listen to people we respect, and we value their opinions. We tend to ignore the opinions and advice of those we don't respect. If you take a moment to think about someone you very much respect, you will find that she exerted considerable influence over you. When people respect us, they listen to us, and we have influence over them—and this applies in our families, communities, and workplaces. Look at the relationship between parents and their teenage children. Is there anything that makes the parents' blood boil more than their children's disregarding, disobeying, or dismissing them?

Leaders depend on the power derived from respect. Leaders are only powerful to the extent that they influence many followers to act in ways to further their vision. Martin Luther King, Jr. was powerful because he influenced millions of followers to support his vision of civil rights. (If you think you're a great leader, but when you look over your shoulder, you don't see anyone, that's a problem.) So, if you want to be followed, you need to be respected. When leaders lose the respect of others, they lose followers and, subsequently, power. People don't listen to them anymore. Sadly, there are frequent examples in the media that make this point. Joe Paterno, the legendary Penn State football coach, lost the respect of nearly everyone and was completely shunned for something he *didn't* do—namely, appropriately reporting child sexual abuse. After admitting to steroid use, the world's most decorated cyclist, Lance Armstrong, was stripped of his Olympic medals and lost the admiration and respect of millions. The enormously respected four-star general David Petraeus was forced to resign as the head of the CIA when his extramarital affair was made public. When you lose others' respect, you lose followers, and you lose power. And it happens in the blink of an eye.

On Your Playing Field

We encourage you to carefully consider the role that respect plays in your life and how you may be able to garner greater respect. In Appendix A we share 42 SuperTips for earning the respect of your team members. We encourage you to select a few of these behaviors and begin incorporating them into your interactions with others. By the way, the most effective strategy is also the most basic: to get respect, you've got to give it!

Wrap-Up

We believe that respect is central to survival in the world and the workplace.

Team members viewed as highly skilled garner respect and—for the most part—enjoy job security. Less skilled and less productive employees are seen as having less value to the team and, thus, as being expendable. How respected are you?

Up Next

In the next chapter, we will take on the issue of respect in the workplace and examine different forms of respect, the extent to which you are respected on your team, the cost of disrespect, and specific behaviors that demonstrate respect.

CHAPTER 3 Respect in the Workplace

> Probably no greater honor can come to any man
> than the respect of his colleagues.
>
> —*Cary Grant*

Overview

If you're still reading, we're going to assume that you agree with us that respect is critical to human relationships, and you can see that it is the necessary foundation for a SuperTeam. The RESPECT Model's underlying thesis that *relationships work only within the context of respect* is so basic, universal, and self-evident that neither of us can recall ever being challenged on it. And when people respect one another, they engage, and when they disrespect one another or feel disrespected, they disengage.

In this chapter, you will learn:

- Different forms of respect
- Characteristics associated with people we respect
- The impact of disrespect in the workplace
- Specific behaviors that demonstrate respect and disrespect
- Tips for dealing with bullies

SUPERSTARTER QUESTIONS

1. Think about someone you greatly respect. What is it about this individual that has you hold him or her in such high esteem?
2. Can you think of someone for whom you have lost respect? What were the circumstances that caused your opinion of this individual to change, and how did it impact your relationship?
3. Have you ever lost respect for someone but that person earned it back? What did it take to regain your respect?
4. How does someone earn respect?
5. Are you treated with respect by your team members and team leader?

RESPECT SELF-ASSESSMENT

Instructions: Read each statement below, and, using the following scale, decide how accurately it describes your team:

Strongly disagree: 0 points
Disagree: 1 point
Agree: 2 points
Strongly agree: 3 points

Place the point value of your answer choice on the blank line at the beginning of each of the following statements:

_____ 1. **Your skills and talents are valued by your team leader.**
_____ 2. **Team members value your suggestions and opinions.**
_____ 3. **Your team members have your back.**
_____ 4. **You are given opportunities to learn and grow.**
_____ 5. **You have autonomy in how to complete your tasks, and you are trusted to make your own decisions.**

_____ **Total score**

INTERPRETING YOUR SCORES

0 to 5: Your experience of disrespect is significant, and you may feel ostracized and perhaps even targeted. You and your work are not appreciated, and you have little, if any, influence with your team members and the decisions made. You are likely concerned—and rightfully so—about your job security. Why do you think that others don't respect you? Are there things that you have done or said—or not done—that have led others to view you as incompetent or as a TeamMe player? Do you feel that others are jealous of you? We encourage you to have some serious and authentic conversations with yourself and then with your coworkers to better understand these issues.

6 to 10: It is likely that you feel respected by some team members but not by others. You respect those who show you respect, and, thus, you engage and work collaboratively with those individuals. Reflect on the history of your relationships with those in the disrespect category. Did respect ever exist? If so, what incident or incidents caused that to change? (Typically, there is one specific trigger event.) Regardless of how long ago the incidents occurred, we recommend that you take responsibility for cleaning up the relationships and initiate a conversation with those individuals. If you don't the relationships will not change and yours will not be a SuperTeam.

11 to 15: You feel respected by and you respect those on your team. You feel connected to and engaged with your fellow team members and team leader. Such relationships lead to regular communication, collaboration, and mutual support, which results in high team functioning and effectiveness. Appreciate these relationships, but don't take them for granted. Continue to foster a culture of respect in your organization. Can you use the influence that comes with respect to improve interpersonal conflict between other team members?

ASSESSMENT REFLECTION EXERCISE

Based on the results of the self-assessment exercise, consider the following questions:

1. How satisfied are you with the level of respect that your team members show to you?

2. Whom do you respect the most on your team?
3. Why do you respect this person?
4. Whom do you disrespect the most on your team?
5. Why do you disrespect this person?
6. Usually, the people we don't respect also don't respect us. What can you do to garner greater respect from a team member who disrespects you? (See Appendix A.)

Qualities of People We Respect

On both a personal and professional level, we respect people for many different reasons. Below is a list of frequently cited qualities and characteristics. As you read each, identify those that you think most of your team members would say you possess and demonstrate:

_____ Accomplished
_____ Authentic, genuine
_____ Available
_____ Compassionate, empathic
_____ Competent
_____ Committed, dedicated
_____ Confident
_____ Courageous
_____ Determined, driven
_____ Disciplined
_____ Enthusiastic
_____ Ethical, moral
_____ Fair
_____ Generous
_____ Grateful
_____ Honest
_____ Honorable
_____ Humble, modest
_____ Integrity
_____ Kind
_____ Listens
_____ Loyal

_____ Mentors, teaches
_____ Nurturing
_____ Open-minded, flexible
_____ Passionate
_____ Patient
_____ Positive, optimistic
_____ Rational
_____ Reliable
_____ Responsible, accountable
_____ Responsive
_____ Selfless
_____ Sensitive
_____ Self-sacrificing
_____ Seeks to understand others' perspectives
_____ Strong work ethic
_____ Supportive
_____ Trustworthy
_____ Understanding
_____ Walk the talk
_____ Wise

On Your Playing Field

As you know by now, being highly respected leads to good things like being valued by others and being influential. So, how to garner more respect should be on your mind throughout this book. From the preceding list, identify three qualities that you would like to work on. Now the important part: identify at least one behavior that would demonstrate this quality to others. For example, if you're one of those people who are always complaining and need to be more positive, you could actually come into the office and say some-thing—anything—positive, such as "What a nice day it is." It's really that easy, and, yes, it really makes a difference. If you need to be more responsive, commit to replying to all e-mails and voice mails within 24 hours—or sooner depending on the culture of your orga-nization. If you cannot reply to an e-mail within that time frame, the respectful action is to let the other person know when you will be able to fully respond. If you don't normally ask others for their opin-ion, start doing so!

Engaging in new behaviors never feels natural—if it did, you'd already be doing them! What is most critical as you go about engag-ing in new behaviors is that you do so sincerely and authentically. If you're just trying to fool those around you, the only person you'll be fooling is yourself. Also, don't expect people to start coming out of the woodwork and immediately recognize these changes. You need to be consistent before others believe that you've really changed—and they should hesitate.

Two Types of Respect: Interpersonal and Technical

When we talk about respecting people, we hold them in high esteem and regard. We listen to such people, and they influence our thoughts, behaviors, and decisions, and we likely show defer-ence to them. In the workplace, we generally respect those who keep their word, support their fellow team members, treat others kindly, remain open to the perspectives and opinions of others, and put the interests of the team above their own. We judge such individuals as "good" people and as TeamWe players.

A second important dimension of respect is the extent to which we respect individuals' technical skills and their ability to "get the job done." People can readily make the distinction between technical and interpersonal respect. On a SuperTeam, team members respect one another on both fronts. Unfortunately, it is relatively common for people to only half respect their coworkers.

Bob and Carol work in the IT department of their organization. Technically speaking, Bob is excellent, and Carol recognizes this. She can trust Bob to do his job. However, she has little interpersonal respect for him. He is arrogant and condescending. He regularly bad-mouths team members behind their backs while bragging about his own accomplishments. He is quick to point the finger when things go wrong and even quicker to take the credit when things go well. Bob is a TeamMe player.

What is the impact of Bob's behavior and Carol's lack of respect for him? Obviously, there is little, if any, sense of collaboration as Carol does whatever she can to avoid Bob—even if it means not getting information that she needs. More broadly, those in other parts of the organization view the IT department as dysfunctional. There is likely a loss of respect in the team leader who apparently is unable to or unwilling to control Bob's behavior. Team members do not hold Bob accountable because they know it will do nothing, and it may actually lead to retribution, which they are afraid of. Bob is allowed to roam freely as the rest of his team members and the quality of their work suffers.

Let's switch the scenario. Imagine Bob as an extremely affable and friendly individual who takes an active interest in Carol and is considerate, thoughtful, and supportive toward all team members. Bob is always willing to help her and others out. Unfortunately, his "help" is typically not helpful. As nice as he is, and as much as everyone wants to see Bob succeed, he just doesn't have the skills. Others may well try to help educate Bob and may even cover for him, but at some point, his fellow team members must concede that Bob simply isn't an asset and he is bringing down the team. Customers begin requesting "anyone but Bob," leading to the workload being inequitably distributed. Bob's work has to be continually checked because others can't trust its accuracy. Frustration becomes widespread within his team and with customers. By the way, just as you do, we feel bad for the Bobs of this world who are set up to fail when they are tasked with responsibilities for which they are not qualified.

When team members disrespect one another on either a technical or interpersonal level, the work of the team suffers. People deceive themselves when they think they can work effectively with someone they don't respect. The examples highlight the two principal reasons why it is **impossible** for team members who don't fully respect one another on both the technical and interpersonal fronts to function effectively. First, whenever we lose respect for people or they lose respect for us, there is always a profound breakdown in communication. We simply don't want to engage with them. Second, when we don't respect people, we usually don't trust them either. If you don't respect people's technical skills, you don't trust them to get the job done, and you end up checking their work. If you don't respect people on an interpersonal level, you don't trust them to have your back. In fact, you keep watching your back to make sure they aren't putting a knife in it. When we don't trust people, we always keep them at arm's length, and we are suspicious of their intentions and actions.

When disrespect enters a relationship, communication and trust go out the window.

Assessing Respect

We determine whether we respect others and feel respected by them based on our observations and interpretation of their behavior— or lack of behavior. We also make assumptions and create stories regarding the intentions behind these behaviors—we attempt to become mind readers. Whether a particular behavior is considered respectful or disrespectful can be extremely subjective; indeed, as we'll see, agreeing on what constitutes disrespectful behaviors is particularly challenging. Let's begin by focusing on respectful workplace behaviors.

Respectful Workplace Behaviors

When you talk about the importance of showing respect in the workplace, people's heads nod up and down. They get it. You get it. What is so surprising then is the difficulty that many people have in identifying more than a few behaviors. (We have a list of more than a hundred ways to show respect to others, and we would be happy to e-mail the list to you. Just send a note to Paul at Paul@PaulMarciano .com.) Grab a piece of paper and give yourself five minutes to write down as many behaviors as you can. (Don't cheat and look ahead— people don't respect cheaters!) Ready? Go.

Now please take a look at our top 25 list. How did you do?

1. Be punctual to meetings and considerate of others' time.
2. Give credit to those who deserve it.
3. Be supportive of others' ideas during meetings.
4. Encourage your fellow team members to share their suggestions and opinions.
5. Give your full attention to others when they are speaking.
6. Ask people if they would like to be put on or remain on an e-mail distribution list.
7. Ask team members appropriate questions about their personal lives—for example, "How old are your children?"
8. Ask another team member for advice.
9. Ask a team member how you could help him or her.
10. Invite someone you don't know well out for lunch.
11. Be patient and give others the time they need to reflect on an issue, ask questions, share their thoughts, or come to a decision.
12. Give "straight" feedback in a supportive and constructive manner.
13. Give people as much advance notice as possible when assignments are due or meetings are to take place.
14. Leave an appreciative or congratulatory note on someone's desk.
15. Let other meeting participants know in advance if you will be late, if you will have to leave early, or if you will have to take an urgent call.
16. Introduce yourself to someone from another team.

17. Ask a team member to give you feedback on your performance.
18. Apologize when you've made a mistake.
19. Seek to understand others' perspectives—especially when you disagree.
20. When presenting your ideas, say, "I'd like to offer my perspective."
21. Let others know that you've been actively listening by saying, "Let me be sure I understand your point of view."
22. Respond promptly to e-mails and phone calls.
23. Ask people their preferred mode of communication—for example, in person, by telephone, or by e-mail.
24. Talk to people, not about people.
25. The basics: hold the door open; say "please" and "thank you"; say "good morning," "have a nice evening," and "I hope you have a nice weekend"; look people in the eye when you speak to them; and clean up after yourself!

On Your Playing Field

Creating a respectful workplace starts with you. Look back at both our list and yours, and circle three behaviors that you could do more often. (If you're having trouble identifying these behaviors, ask your team members—preferably those with whom you don't have a great relationship.) Now, here comes the most important part: get a yellow sticky note and write down these behaviors. Place the note in your work space where you will easily and frequently see it; you want this prompt to be "in your face." (Most frequently people affix the note to the bottom of their computer monitor. If a yellow sticky or computer monitor doesn't work for you, figure out what does.) The note will serve as a prompt, and prompts are critical when you're trying to change or engage in new behaviors.

Another effective strategy is to put reminders in your calendar for either the beginning or end of the day. Your challenge is to engage in each of these behaviors at least three times a week. Tracking and recording your efforts will make them more likely to occur, as will making a public declaration of your intentions to others. Keep at it for three months, at which point, hopefully, these behaviors will have turned into habits. Then consider taking on another set of behaviors. By the way, you'll know if you're being successful because others will begin to relate to you and treat you with more respect.

Disrespectful Workplace Behaviors

When it comes to defining disrespectful workplace behaviors, things get fuzzy. Consider the following examples. Sam thinks he receives more work than his colleagues. Shona believes that she is held to a higher standard than the rest of her team. Rick doesn't feel respected because no one asks for his opinion. Jack didn't like the tone of voice a team member used with him. John didn't get the big account that he thought he deserved. Carol got sent to a training class when Barb thinks that she deserved the opportunity. Are these examples of disrespectful workplace behaviors? Maybe. Maybe not. Disrespect lies in the eye of the individual, and it depends on many factors that are largely subjective. We beg you—in both your personal and professional life—to not tell people who feel upset or disrespected that they "shouldn't feel that way." People have every right to feel any way they want, and you need to respect that.

Unintentional Acts of Disrespect

It is often what people don't do that leads others to believe they are disrespectful. When someone fails to say "thank you," ignores our hard work, or walks by without saying "hello," we take offense even though that person likely had no intention of making us feel this way.

Paul had a long-standing engagement with an organization, and over time he had gotten to know the office staff on a first-name basis. Whenever he met with the human resources manager, he walked by their cubicles. One day the manager said, "Paul, I've got something awkward to tell you. Some of the staff don't think you are being respectful toward them." Well, there's not much worse that you can say to Paul! The staff was upset because he did not make a point of going around and saying hello to each of them when he came in. They felt that Paul was ignoring them and being rude. Paul's motivation? He thought he was respecting them by not disturbing them!

Whether it is your intention or not, at times, you are going to act in ways that others will interpret as disrespectful. At the end of the day, the interpretation and impact of the behavior trumps the intent. Of course, actually confronting the individuals has the potential to clean up the issue. The problem is that the people who are offended rarely say anything—at least to the person they feel offended by. Has it ever happened to you that months after something happened, it came out that your behavior offended someone? Without the problem being brought to the other person's attention, it cannot be addressed, and often leads to the other person harboring resentment.

Paul once worked with a high-potential assistant manager, Mike, who, while giving a presentation felt publicly berated by his manager, Jim—at least that's how he perceived it. He felt embarrassed and disrespected in front of his team. Mike shared this incident with Paul who suggested that he had two options. First, do nothing and be resentful. Second, bring it up to his manager. The second is clearly the better option—as long as it is done in a respectful and tactful manner. After some coaching, Mike asked to speak to his manager and said, "Jim, I am wondering if you were really disappointed with how I handled that last project." Jim responded, "Not at all. Why would you think that?" Mike referred to the meeting and his boss's comments, and then he told him how he interpreted those comments. Mike did not accuse Jim of intentionally disrespecting him, he just stated what was said and how it made him feel. Jim responded, "Mike, I'm really sorry. That was not at all my intention. I had just come from a very stressful meeting, and I took it out on you."

At the next team meeting, Jim publicly acknowledged Mike for all his hard work and apologized for appearing so critical of him during the previous meeting. A situation that could have resulted in long-term resentment was easily resolved because Mike had the courage to step up and speak with his boss. By the way, because of how Jim responded, he gained the respect of not only Mike but also the rest of the team. Take responsibility to hold these conversations, or let go of feeling sorry for yourself.

The following list contains behaviors that are nearly always agreed upon as disrespectful and should be avoided. And, we will tell you that even some of these behaviors can be found to be perfectly acceptable in some organizational cultures.

1. Gossiping
2. Arriving late to meetings
3. Accusing and pointing fingers at others
4. Berating others—especially in public
5. Bragging about personal accomplishments and achievements
6. Dictating to others what they must do or how they must do it
7. Being condescending and demeaning
8. Withholding or providing misleading information
9. Inappropriately copying or blind copying others on e-mails
10. Dismissing and criticizing another's opinion
11. Ignoring or ostracizing others
12. Taking credit for another's work
13. Failing to take responsibility for one's mistakes
14. Failing to follow through on commitments
15. Being hypocritical—saying one thing and doing another
16. Being inattentive—for example, looking at one's phone during meetings
17. Interrupting others
18. Invading others' privacy or personal space
19. Jumping to conclusions; being presumptuous
20. Raising one's voice; yelling
21. Rambling and dominating conversations
22. Making unreasonable requests of others
23. Being unresponsive to the others' requests
24. Using vulgar language or physical gestures
25. Lying or misrepresenting the facts

How many of these behaviors regularly occur on your team? None? Five? Ten? All of them? As the number of regularly occurring disrespectful behaviors on your team increases, the more disrespect is part of your culture and the more difficult it will be to change.

As always, take responsibility for being a role model and part of the solution, not the problem.

Bullying Behavior

Bullying is an extreme form of disrespect characterized by a persistent pattern of behaviors that threaten, intimidate, degrade, undermine, embarrass, and humiliate others. The prevalence of bullying and its negative impact on individuals and organizations is staggering. A survey from the nonprofit organization Workplace Bullying Institute found that 35 percent of workers have experienced bullying firsthand—making bullying the most common type of harassment. Fifty percent of people report either experiencing or witnessing such behavior. Any behavior or event that adversely impacts one out of every two people isn't a problem, it is an epidemic.

The Bully

Most people don't think of themselves as jerks. They often don't view their behavior as problematic at all. Bullies say that they aren't yelling; they are just "passionate" about their work. Bullies say that their victims are overly sensitive or take things the wrong way. Bullies often feel superior to their coworkers and manager. They believe that they work harder, they are smarter, and they have higher standards than others. Although there are exceptions, most individuals aren't intentionally being bullies. (Unfortunately, there are a handful of individuals who derive pleasure and take pride in abusing others. We strongly suggest avoiding such individuals.)

Bullies have significant blind spots when it comes to the appropriateness of their behavior. In the toolbox of human resources professionals, the 360-degree assessment is one of the most powerful and usually the most effective way to open the bully's eyes and make him or her amenable to coaching. When bullies receive feedback based on the RESPECT 360-degree assessment, they are typically shocked by how low others have scored them; they typically score themselves at the very top of the scale. The individuals frequently get upset—which is a good sign. If they say, "Oh well," then you've got a very serious problem on your hands. As you might expect, there is a high correlation between the extent to which people are viewed as treating others respectfully and the extent to which they are respected. It is also extremely interesting to note that there exists a strong correlation between the extent to which individuals are respected and their perceived level of effectiveness—regardless of any objective metrics of effectiveness. When we don't respect others or don't feel respected by them, we also don't view them as effective in their role.

Why Is Such Behavior Tolerated?

The most common reason that bullies are not held accountable for their behavior and sternly reprimanded or terminated is that they are viewed as too valuable to the organization either because of their technical skills or revenue generation. Unfortunately, it is our experience that such individuals get a slap on the wrist, and while they may act more appropriately for a short while, they always return to their old ways. Sadly, instead of the bully being held accountable, the victim often quits or is even terminated. When this happens, the bully becomes even more emboldened, and team members become more vulnerable. Unfortunately, we have many unbelievable stories. At the risk of offending the reader, the following is one of our favorites: one team member urinated in another team member's lunch box. You would think this kind of behavior would result in termination. His manager told him to stop acting like such an ass and then promoted him to assistant manager two months later.

Ideally, the rest of the team confronts this individual and lets him or her know that this behavior will no longer be tolerated. Realistically, this seldom happens—and possibly for a good reason. We have seen cases in which brave individuals have stood up to the bully on the behalf of others, but it turned out very poorly for these virtuous team members as they became the target of the bully.

With the support of the human resources department, the team leaders are fully responsible for dealing with these bullying individuals. Unfortunately, the team leaders may actually feel threatened and be unwilling to say anything for fear of provoking the bullies. Frequently, the team leaders simply don't have the skills to deal effectively with such individuals. In the worst-case scenarios, the team leaders are the bullies or they actually approve of and reinforce such behavior! If you have a boss who believes in motivating through intimidation and fear, it is probably best to start looking for another team.

SuperTips for Bullying Victims

1. Nip bullying in the bud! As soon as you feel bullied, confront the individual, and let him or her know in no uncertain terms that you will not tolerate such behavior. When confronted with conviction, bullies often back down and, unfortunately, redirect their venom toward someone else.

2. Document and keep a record of the bullying behaviors— for example, a diary of the incidents, e-mails, voice mails, and written statements by coworkers who observed the behaviors. After collecting such evidence take the following actions:
   - Call a meeting with the individual's manager and human resources, and provide specific examples and documentation of the unacceptable behaviors.
   - Push for accountability and specific actions to be taken if the behaviors continue.
   - Ask the question, "How would you like me to respond to such behavior going forward?"
   - Write a summary of what was discussed, and e-mail it to human resources and the manager.

3. Do whatever you can to keep your interactions with the person public so that others can witness and validate how you are being treated.

4. Seek professional counseling to help you cope with the stress.

5. If the bullying continues, consider getting legal representation.

On Your Playing Field

We certainly hope that you are not a victim of bullying in the workplace; however, if you feel that you are being bullied by a team member or your team leader, we strongly encourage you to consider our SuperTips. If you witness the bullying of a fellow team member, you may want to pass this list along to that person. If doing so directly is uncomfortable, you may just want to type up the list and drop it off at the victim's desk.

Wrap-Up

Disrespect always leads to dysfunction. When individuals feel disrespected and bullied, there are profound consequences for them, the team, the organization, and the customers. Unfortunately, bullies are rarely held accountable for their actions. Teams don't function when team members don't treat one another with respect. There is simply no place for disrespect, and certainly not bullying, on a SuperTeam. What can you do to encourage respect and discourage disrespect on your team?

Up Next

Having laid the groundwork for the relationship between respect and team functioning, we will introduce the RESPECT Model and the specific factors that contribute to a culture of team respect. Now we're getting to the good stuff!

PART II

The RESPECT Model

Every human being, of whatever origin, of whatever station, deserves respect. We must each respect others even as we respect ourselves.
—*Ralph Waldo Emerson*

As previously discussed, SuperTeams require employees who are highly engaged with both their work and coworkers, and that happens only in an environment of mutual respect. Teams are composed of a network of relationships; when disrespect is present in any of those relationships, the functioning of the team suffers. The extent to which team members experience respect is determined largely by the seven key drivers of the RESPECT Model. This acronym and its meaning are the same as were presented in Paul's book *Carrots and Sticks Don't Work:*

Recognition
Empowerment
Supportive feedback
Partnering
Expectations
Consideration
Trust

This book, *SuperTeams*, frames each of these drivers within the context of the team and emphasizes the responsibility of each team member for creating a culture of respect through his or her actions.

Embrace the hell out of personal responsibility.
—*Mike Krzyzewski, Coach, Duke University*

CHAPTER 4 Recognition

> Don't worry when you are not recognized, but strive
> to be worthy of recognition.
>
> —*Abraham Lincoln*

Overview

There are few findings in the behavioral sciences better documented than the extraordinary impact of reinforcement on human behavior. The most powerful form of reinforcement is recognition through praise. When we receive recognition from our team members, we feel validated and appreciated, and we also feel more secure. Despite the overwhelming evidence demonstrating the critical role of recognition and the ease with which it can be shown, it is simply remarkable that we pay so little attention to giving attention.

In this chapter, you will learn:

- The extent to which your team appropriately recognizes the contributions of its team members
- The impact of recognizing and failing to recognize the work of others
- Some of the barriers to recognition
- Specific tips on how to deliver powerful recognition

As a starting point, take a moment to reflect on the following questions.

SUPERSTARTER QUESTIONS

1. When was the last time you gave kudos to another team member, and what was the reason for doing so?
2. When was the last time you received a "thanks" or "good job" from another team member or team leader?
3. Think about a time when you really went above and beyond on a project and no one said anything. How did it make you feel? How did it affect your level of motivation?
4. How does your organization recognize a team's accomplishments?
5. What can you do to foster a culture in which team members' work is appreciated?

RECOGNITION TEAM ASSESSMENT

Instructions: Read each statement below, and, using the following scale, decide how accurately it describes your team:

Strongly disagree: 0 points
Disagree: 1 point
Agree: 2 points
Strongly agree: 3 points

Place the point value of your answer choice on the blank line at the beginning of each of the following statements:

____ **1. Team members are appropriately recognized for their contributions.**

____ **2. Team members are rewarded based on their work performance.**

____ **3. The team leader recognizes team members who help improve the team.**

____ **4. The team as a whole is recognized for meeting critical milestones.**

____ **5. Team members acknowledge and show appreciation for one another's contributions.**

____ **Total score**

INTERPRETING YOUR SCORES

0 to 5: If your team is underperforming and there is low morale, the profound lack of recognition is likely a major factor. Team members do not feel acknowledged for their work at an individual or group level. They feel that their work is not valued or appreciated, and they feel taken for granted and disrespected. The only time people get recognized is when they screw up. Unless this issue is addressed at all levels—that is, by team members, team leaders, and team sponsors—there is little hope that your team will ever achieve SuperTeam status.

6 to 10: Your team's mediocre recognition score likely contributes to a "show up and do my job" attitude and concomitant level of effort. Team members have little expectation that working hard will lead to any monetary or nonmonetary rewards. Little appreciation leads to little inspiration. Without improvement in this area, moderately engaged team members will continue to deliver moderate results.

11 to 15: Scores in this range suggest that team members are regularly acknowledged by their team leader and by one another and their work is appreciated by the organization. Team members feel valued and are more likely to be engaged and to contribute higher levels of discretionary effort. When hard work is reinforced, people work harder. Morale is likely high, and team members feel positively toward one another, their team leader, and organization.

ASSESSMENT REFLECTION EXERCISE

We would like you to reflect on the relationship between recognition, respect, and engagement:

1. Think about the job where you felt that your contributions were most valued and appropriately recognized. Did you feel respected? Yes or no?
2. On a scale from 1 (not at all) to 10 (extremely so), how would you rate your level of engagement while in this job?
3. Think about the job where you felt that your contributions were least valued and appropriately recognized. Did you feel respected? Yes or no?
4. On a scale from 1 (not at all) to 10 (extremely so), how would you rate your level of engagement?

If you're like most people, including us, you found that in jobs where you were recognized for your contributions, you felt respected and were significantly more engaged than in those jobs in which you did not feel acknowledged for your contributions.

The Power of Recognition

The concept is simple and the research is clear: whether in personal or professional relationships, when people feel appreciated, they engage. Even for people who say that they don't care about being acknowledged, when they are acknowledged, their engagement increases. The problem is that people with this "I don't need it" attitude often resent and resist the idea that others should need such reinforcement to "do their job." Such team members typically come across as curmudgeonly, superior, and critical, and they have a markedly negative impact on team morale and functioning.

When team members, the team leader, the team sponsor, and customers take the time to say "thank you," people work harder. And they feel better about the work they do and the people they work with.

Pay close attention to what behavior you are recognizing and rewarding, and make sure that it is not having unintended consequences. For example, if you choose to reward only productivity, you may actually reduce quality and safety compliance. You are better off paying attention to the behaviors that lead to your desired outcomes such as more and better teamwork, communication, resourcefulness, and initiative taking. Moreover, you should be strategic in which behaviors you reinforce for different team members. Always look for the behavior that, if improved, would have the biggest impact on that individual and the team. For example, Clinton may be excellent at mentoring more junior team members, and doing so has an extremely positive impact on the team; however, he doesn't often take the time to do so. Thus, whenever you see Clinton engaging in such behavior, you would want to make sure to say something positive.

The Power of Ignoring

We often engage in behavior to the benefit of others without receiving any kind of thanks or recognition. Have you ever had a team member or boss who constantly asked you to rush a job, but rarely took the time to sincerely thank you for doing so? When behavior is ignored or not authentically praised, it is a whole lot less likely to occur in the future. (Obviously, there are times that we very much want to extinguish behavior, and ignoring it is highly effective. A case in point would be the whiny team member who harps on everything that is wrong. Unfortunately, we often unintentionally reinforce such behavior by simply listening politely.) We are not talking about jumping up and down when someone does us a favor. We are talking about looking that person in the eye and saying, "Thank you." A few words can have an enormous impact on that individual and his future behavior.

Imagine a man sending his wife, partner, or significant other a dozen long-stem red roses (or other favorite flower or candy). He is not giving this gift for a specific occasion, nor is he in the proverbial doghouse. He just does so as a loving gesture. Now imagine that his partner says nothing. The question is: When is the next time he will bring home such an unexpected gift? Paul's favorite response to this question came during a workshop in Alabama when a gentleman with a thick southern drawl responded, "At her gravesite."

Whether it is your significant other, your child, or a team member, failing to recognize another's efforts and gestures will invariably lead to a decline in that person's initiative to engage in such behavior again. By the way, the generally accepted notion that we can change only our own behavior and not that of others is simply and wholly wrong. We are *constantly* changing the behaviors of those around us by how we consciously and unconsciously respond to them, and vice versa.

Why Are We So Bad at Giving Praise?

Such behavior—or lack of behavior—is consistent with the general principle that human beings are not wired to pay attention to what is working. Instead, we are wired to pay attention to what is not working. From an evolutionary perspective, this makes a lot of sense. We can't pay attention to everything going on in our world. Thus, when things are "normal" or "right," we tend not to notice them. Only when situations are not what we expect do our brains put up a red flag. When was the last time you turned on your computer and said, "Great, it works!"? Probably not since the last time you had a problem with your computer working. Team members who don't fulfill their obligations get noticed a lot more than those who do. Doing a lousy job often elicits more attention than doing a great job. By the way, harping on the behavior you don't want rarely gets you the behavior that you do want. Nagging is not an effective behavior modification strategy.

The RESPECT Model is an actionable philosophy—it is about acting in ways that actually demonstrate respect. The following story is not shared to show what a nice guy Paul is, but rather to be an example of how to bring the concepts of RESPECT, and specifically recognition, to life in your world and the impact doing so can have.

Arriving an hour before his bus was scheduled to depart the Port Authority in New York City, Paul decided to grab a bite to eat. He was seated at a table in a nearly empty restaurant located at the entrance to the Port Authority building. Bill, a middle-aged gentleman, appeared and cheerfully introduced himself as Paul's server and quipped about the unseasonably warm weather. He asked Paul in a most sincere manner how his day was going, and he seemed pleased that his customer was having a fine day. Bill then humorously shared the day's specials. When the food arrived, he said that he hoped Paul liked it—and he meant it. And if he didn't, he would be happy to get him something else. While handing Paul the check, he thanked Paul for coming in and wished him a good trip. (Paul was struck, sadly, by the unusually good service. He also realized that as a young man, Bill probably did not aspire to be a waiter in a restaurant located in the Port Authority, and, thus, Paul's respect and appreciation of Bill's exceptional service increased all the more.)

When Paul received the check, he wrote on the bottom, "Bill, thanks for your positive energy and humor. You really made my day." From where Paul was seated, he saw Bill take the check over to the cash register. When he opened the check, he noticed Paul's note; you could literally see the surprise on his face. (Apparently this doesn't happen every day to waiters in New York City.) He then did something Paul will always remember. Want to guess what that was? Bill walked over and showed the receipt to his manager who said, "That is really nice. You should keep it." Let that sink in. Really sink in. How could it be that such a simple gesture coming from a total stranger could mean so much? Every day we have opportunities to say "thank you" to our friends, family members, coworkers, customers, and total strangers. Let people know that you appreciate the contribution they are making to you.

Showing Recognition

As a team member or leader, there are several simple ways to acknowledge people—some more effective than others, depending on the individual. Examples include writing a thank you note, giving a "shout-out" via e-mail or preferably during a team meeting, taking the person for coffee, sending the person flowers, or offering to give the person a hand with his work. By the way, just chatting with people and asking them how things are going—especially on a personal level—can be extremely reinforcing. Team leaders should share their employees' accomplishments with their boss, and they should look to reward hard-working team members with desirable opportunities. On a team level, many organizations use a "recognition wall," where team members regularly give written kudos to one another. What are some other effective ways you've been recognized or you've seen other people be recognized?

Since we're not wired to recognize "good" behavior, we need to figure out how to remind ourselves to do so. The most effective strategy is by using *prompts*. Prompts are physical or auditory reminders to engage in a particular behavior, and they come in many shapes

---

Kudos in the Cloud

As you may know, various online recognition platforms have emerged. Paul is fortunate to be on the board of Kudos whose motto is, "Changing the world one thank you at a time." Kudos is a peer-to-peer recognition program that allows team members to give public or private kudos to one another. Team members located anywhere can give and receive prompt, specific, and meaningful recognition using a fun and engaging platform. When you give kudos, you can choose to do so at different levels; the ability to discriminate reward levels increases the power of the reinforcement.

Another excellent Kudos feature is that it gives users the ability to easily include the characteristics associated with the behavior—for example, "reliable, thoughtful, proactive, and resourceful." This kind of platform allows team members to accrue a permanent record of their endorsements, and it serves as their public reputation. (Similarly, LinkedIn allows its users to endorse others in their network for specific skills.) Finally, you can even set the Kudos system up to prompt you to deliver this feedback! (For more information, visit www.kudosnow.com.)

---

and sizes. The most common examples include some form of a written note, a calendar reminder, an alarm clock, and the old rubber band on the wrist. Paul once had a desk plaque made for a client that said: "Who helped me out today?" Another strategy is to ask others to remind you to engage in the new behavior. For example, you might ask a fellow team member to point out when she sees someone who deserves a pat on the back.

On Your Playing Field

Identify individuals on your team who deserve some recognition. If you really want to make a difference, select people who are frequently overlooked or people with whom you may not have a close relationship. For better or worse, praise often has more impact when it comes from someone we don't know well or with whom we have been in conflict. In the next week, find a simple way to show your gratitude to others.

Wrap-Up

When people are acknowledged for their contributions, they feel valued and respected, which increases their level of engagement to the team and work. When we recognize behavior, we get more of it. When we ignore it, we get less of it. A simple "thank you" can have a profound impact on others, and opportunities to express our gratitude exist all around us. In the workplace, SuperTeams have a Kudos culture.

Up Next

Recognition is typically reserved for times when people go above and beyond—that is, when they exceed our expectations. Team members are in the best position to do so when they are fully empowered. In the next chapter, we will discuss empowerment and how it is used to create a SuperTeam.

CHAPTER 5 # Empowerment

> An empowered organization is one in which
> individuals have the knowledge, skill, desire, and
> opportunity to personally succeed in a way that
> leads to collective organizational success.
>
> —*Stephen Covey*

Overview

SuperTeams can exist only with highly empowered team members. Such employees are not only skilled in their specific job responsibilities, but they are also cross-trained to support other team players, they are given autonomy and decision-making authority by their team leader, and they are encouraged to think outside the box and to take educated risks. The more empowered a team member, the greater an asset he is to the team. Unfortunately, it is the rare team, yes, the SuperTeam, in which all team members are fully empowered and enabled to deliver their very best.

In this chapter, you will learn:

- The extent to which your team is empowered
- What empowerment is and what it looks like on the playing field
- Some of the barriers to team member empowerment
- How to create an empowerment culture
- Specific empowerment tips

As a starting point, take a moment to reflect on the following questions.

SUPERSTARTER QUESTIONS

1. Think about a supervisor who really empowered you and allowed you to do your very best. In what specific ways did he empower you?
2. Would you describe your team as empowered? Why?
3. What are the benefits of an empowered team?
4. What keeps teams from being more empowered?
5. How can you more fully empower yourself?

EMPOWERMENT TEAM ASSESSMENT

Instructions: Read each statement below, and, using the following scale, decide how accurately it describes your team:

Strongly disagree: 0 points
Disagree: 1 point
Agree: 2 points
Strongly agree: 3 points

Place the point value of your answer choice on the blank line at the beginning of each of the following statements:

_____ 1. **Team members have sufficient resources to achieve their goals—for example, time, expertise, training, budget, tools, and access to information.**

_____ 2. **Team members are given considerable decision-making responsibility.**

_____ 3. **Team members are encouraged to take risks and try new ways of doing things.**

_____ 4. **Team members have a lot of autonomy and discretion in how they complete their tasks.**

_____ 5. **The team leader regularly acts on feedback and suggestions from team members.**

_____ **Total score**

INTERPRETING YOUR SCORES

0 to 5: A SuperTeam's success is driven largely by highly empowered team members. More than any other RESPECT driver, empowerment relates directly to a team's ability to effectively and efficiently accomplish their tasks. Teams who score at this level are likely failing to achieve even their basic goals and objectives. Along with being disempowered, your team members are also likely highly disengaged.

6 to 10: An average score on empowerment translates into average performance and engagement. Team members are likely frustrated and feel hamstrung by a lack of resources and autonomy. While team leaders are largely responsible for empowering their team, each team member must take responsibility for empowering himself and support his team members to do the same.

11 to 15: Scores in this range suggest that team members are well positioned to succeed. People have the skills and opportunities to do their best work, and they feel valued and trusted. Team members are actively engaged in finding opportunities to become more educated and to educate other team members. Although a high empowerment score does not guarantee SuperTeam status, it is a necessary condition.

ASSESSMENT REFLECTION EXERCISE

SuperTeam members are always in the process of continuous learning and growth. Unfortunately, this is not the priority in most teams. What skills and responsibilities would further your career development? Request a meeting with your team leader to discuss your professional goals and how they fit with the needs of the team and to identify specific opportunities to grow and develop. You may also want to consider contacting the human resources department which may have information regarding additional resources and educational programs.

What Is Empowerment?

To quote human resources expert Susan Heathfield: "Empowerment is the process of enabling or authorizing an individual to think, behave, take action, and control work and decision making in autonomous ways." Other factors such as providing clear expectations and ongoing feedback are also essential parts of empowering a team and will be examined on their own as separate drivers of the RESPECT Model.

Over the past decade there has been increasing attention given to empowering employees. Like most "best practices" in human resources, great organizations and leaders have always worked to empower their people. As discussed earlier, SuperTeams are composed of highly engaged team members who play full out. However, it is impossible to play full out in any meaningful way if you don't have the skills or opportunities to do so. In fact, a lack of empowerment is not only a significant reason for a team's inability to achieve their goals, but it is also a major driver of employee disengagement. No one likes to feel as though his potential is being limited. Empowered employees have the skills and the opportunity to use them. When team members are empowered, they are much more likely to succeed, and success leads to an increase in self-efficacy, which leads individuals to take initiative. Empowerment breeds empowerment.

Employees Aren't Empowered Just Because You Say They Are

Although organizations are extremely interested in empowering their employees, unfortunately, we have seen few that do it well. Employees aren't empowered just because you say they are. You don't bestow empowerment on team members like a queen knighting a prince. Empowering others does not mean delegating tasks irresponsibly to team members who lack the skills, experience, or decision-making authority to succeed. All too often when a team leader tells someone she is empowered, it usually means, "You are empowered as long as you do it my way." This isn't empowerment. This is maddening.

Just out of college with a marketing degree, Erica landed a job as an account representative for a boutique insurance company. She couldn't wait to get started, and she was full of enthusiasm and ambition.

During the interview she was sold on the promise of many educational and advancement opportunities. From the way the hiring manager made it sound, she would receive several weeks of training to get her up to speed. When she came on board she spent the first two days doing the usual new-hire routine—for example, filling out paperwork, watching videos, getting in the "system," and setting up her cubicle and computer. On the third day her manager, Steve, said, "Ready to get to work?" and he handed her a stack of folders. He said, "Here you go. Read the file on top first because we'll be visiting that client tomorrow, and you need to be prepared."

"Prepared for what exactly?" she thought.

Having a strong work ethic and wanting to make a good impression, she stayed up late into the night studying the client's file and trying to understand the various acronyms and jargon. During the meeting, the client began asking Erica questions—most of which she had no answer for. She was a deer in the headlights. Steve tried to make light of the situation by calling her a "newbie"; neither Erica nor the client were comforted by the comment. Erica felt completely humiliated and discouraged. To his credit, Steve was positive and said, "Don't worry, you'll pick it up." When she inquired about getting some training, he said that they were very busy and needed her help. He would try to find her a class next quarter. Realizing that she was not going to receive much support from her manager, she turned to her team members. Unfortunately, they were all far too busy to sit with her and "hold her hand." Again, she heard, "Don't worry, you'll pick it up."

Fortunately, Erica's story has a happy ending. Two months after she began, the company went through a reorganization, and she was assigned to a new supervisor—Nancy. On the very first day Nancy called Erica into her office and said, "So, tell me about yourself?" She then asked Erica about her experiences so far at the organization. Erica was extremely diplomatic in her reply. Nancy wanted to know about Erica's professional ambitions, and she asked her what kind of training and support she would find helpful. Nancy then reviewed Erica's job description and set clear performance expectations. Realizing that Erica had received no structured training, Nancy arranged for her to take a three-day course on the insurance industry and the role of an account manager. In addition, Nancy set Erica up with a mentor and had her partner with a senior account manager to work on a few accounts together. Nancy's approach is what it looks like to empower new employees and set them up for success.

Resistance to Empowering Employees

There are a number of barriers—mostly excuses—that get in the way of empowering team members. We detail the most prominent:

1. **Resistant team leaders.** Sadly, a frequent roadblock to employee empowerment is the team leader who believes that empowering his people means disempowering himself. He may believe that giving his team members autonomy, decision-making responsibility, and opportunities to learn and grow means that he won't be needed anymore. He fears working himself out of a job. Ironically, such should be his exact goal and is the trademark of a SuperTeam leader. Obviously, the more skilled players you have on your team, the more likely the team is to accomplish its goals. And, as the team succeeds, the team leader often gets additional responsibilities and opportunities. Thus, SuperTeam leaders, do in fact, often work themselves out of a job—and into a better one.
2. **Incompetent team leaders.** Although the concept of empowerment may be simple, actually creating and executing a strategy can be challenging—especially with limited resources. Often, team leaders are told that they need to empower their people without their being given any training in how to do so. As evidence of how uneducated most supervisors are when it comes to empowering their people, consider the following. When we hold empowerment workshops, we regularly ask people to identify specific empowerment strategies used in their organization. The number one answer is to send employees to training; unfortunately, this also tends to be the only answer.
3. **Knee-jerk "we can't afford it" reactions.** Obviously training is an important strategy in educating and empowering employees. When the issue of training comes up,

the knee-jerk reaction of most supervisors is, "We can't afford it"—either in terms of the cost of the training or in the loss of productivity resulting from the absence of the people being trained. Obviously, those organizations that do invest in employee training end up with more productive and efficient team members. By the way, team leaders need training more than anyone else. Almost without exception, supervisors have been promoted into their positions for reasons having nothing to do with being effective in this role; promotions are often based on such factors as an employee's tenure, a degree or professional certification, strong work ethic, or expertise, and not because they are good coaches, effective delegators and communicators, and skilled in building a cohesive team.

Most organizations promote excellent employees into positions of supervision where they fail miserably. If your organization does not have a structured process to prepare high-potential individuals for supervision, it needs one. For over a decade, Paul had the pleasure of working with a firm, E.C. Davis and Associates, which put existing and potential supervisors through an intense three-day course known as the Team Manager Development Center. Participants experience an extremely realistic two-day simulation during which they play the role of a team leader and are put through exercise after exercise to pull out the skills that actually matter in order to be effective in this role.

During the program, participants actively supervise others, lead team meetings, collaborate with other departments, give presentations, deal with equipment breakdowns, manage conflict between team members, delegate tasks, coach team members in new skills, and provide performance feedback. The participants receive extensive feedback, which is used to create a development plan that sets the employees up for success when the opportunity to take on a team leader role presents itself. By the way, as a result of this experience, some participants realize that they do not want to take on supervisory responsibilities, and this may be the most valuable learning of all—for the individuals and their organization. (For more information, visit: www.ecdavis.com.)

Empowerment Strategy

Creating an empowered SuperTeam requires a strategic development plan for individual team members that takes into consideration their professional career goals and the needs of the team. Not having well-established learning and growth opportunities is one of the most commonly cited reasons people give for leaving their organization—especially younger employees. On the organization side, failing to empower employees greatly limits a team's effectiveness. Development planning and empowerment should begin as soon as individuals are hired. The team leader must assess an individual's current skills against the stated job responsibilities and determine what additional training is necessary and how it will be delivered—for example, through peer mentoring, coaching by the supervisor, or classroom training.

As individual employees become more accomplished in their roles, the team leader should look for ways to provide greater autonomy and decision-making responsibility. As the employees' skills and responsibilities grow, they and the team leader should begin to identify possible new roles that both interest the employees and make sense for the organization. Once these roles are identified, the team leader and the employees can create a development plan to prepare the employees to be successful should the opportunities arise. Ultimately, however, it is the responsibility of the individual team members to grow and develop themselves. Obviously your team leader and fellow team members play a critical role, but the buck starts and stops with you.

Empowerment Culture

We mentioned in a previous chapter the importance of culture, and it comes into play big time around this issue of empowerment. Empowered teams exist within only those organizational cultures in which continuous learning and advancement are valued. Some organizations have that type of culture, but most don't. Although you may be in the latter group, there are still numerous ways in which you can and should seek to empower yourself and to help foster a culture of empowerment.

SuperTips for Empowerment

As discussed earlier, most human resources managers and team leaders balk at sending employees off for formal training—even when it is sorely needed. However, training does not have to be expensive or even terribly time-consuming. To paraphrase Tony Robbins, achieving one's goals is more about resourcefulness than resources. There are lots of ways to be resourceful when it comes to empowering employees:

1. Offer cross-training opportunities. On the short list of absolute best practices for any organization in any industry of any size, cross-training ranks near the top. Having team members trained in different job functions allows significantly more flexibility and support when a team member is out or needs additional assistance. Take the initiative to ask other team members to educate you on specific aspects of their job, or take the initiative to reach out and ask other team members if they would like to know more about your work. Even job shadowing can be extremely valuable as team members gain an appreciation and understanding of their coworkers' jobs and typically become better collaborators as a result.

2. Don't ask permission. You're not in the fourth grade, and you don't need a hall pass. As we emphasize throughout this book, the responsibility for creating a SuperTeam begins with you and your commitment to continuous learning and improvement. Take the initiative to identify learning opportunities, and pursue them on your own. Meet with the human resources department, and see what low-cost training classes are available. Then present your team leader with a specific plan that includes how your work will be covered. Of course, there is literally an endless amount to be learned through online courses that are free or extremely inexpensive. And then, there is always reading a book!

3. Audit the team's skills. Conduct an audit of the skills the team needs to effectively accomplish its goals. What expertise is needed, and how much of it? In which areas are you light in terms of talent? Are there areas where there is currently not enough expertise? Do you have the time and internal resources to develop these skills, or will you need to look outside the team? Are you prepared for a smooth transition if a team member leaves—including the team leader? Take the initiative to work with your team leader and fellow team members to address the talent needs of the team and inevitable team member transitions.

4. Take an expert to lunch. Your team and organization are full of expertise. Take advantage of it. Identify individuals with the skills and experience that would help further your career goals and contribute to the team's success. Take them out to lunch, and pick their brain, and ask them to mentor you if possible. If a particular individual isn't able to become your mentor, don't abandon the idea. Instead, find someone who is willing and able to do so because having a mentor is an excellent way to gain knowledge in small bites on an ongoing basis.

5. Establish clear decision-making boundaries and autonomy. Having the authority to control your work and make decisions is an essential part of being empowered. Of course, you have to know the boundaries. Often these are not clear. Request a meeting with your team manager to gain clarity, and be willing to push a bit further if you think you are prepared.

6. Know the why behind the what. It would be difficult to overemphasize the value of knowing why something is done in a particular manner. When you know the why, you are able to make better decisions—which is particularly important when things don't go as planned. If you don't know the why behind what you or your coworkers are doing, take the initiative to find out—not knowing is extremely disempowering.

7. Remove barriers. Identify and take down barriers to becoming more empowered. Obviously, this becomes more difficult if the team leader is the roadblock. One good strategy is to ask your team leader for help. For example, you might say to your team leader, "Paul, I really appreciate being on this team, and I want to do the best job possible. There is something that I could use your help on. . . ."

Proceed to give a specific example of the problem and request. For example, "I've been working with the new release of our software program from corporate, and I keep running into problem after problem. What used to take me 20 minutes to complete now takes me up to an hour. When I call or e-mail the IT support team, I get, 'We're working on it.' I know that they are extremely frustrated and doing the best they can, but in the meantime I keep falling more and more behind in my work. The situation is causing a ripple effect and making other team members miss their deadlines." After stating the problem, you can ask for general help. For example, "Can you give me any ideas for how I might deal with this situation?" Or you might ask your team leader to talk to IT on your behalf. If you have a specific suggestion that would work for you, all the better. For example, "Although it would be only a temporary fix, would you ask IT if I can have access to the previous version of the software?"

On Your Playing Field

The following questions will help you put the concepts and strategies of this chapter into action:

1. Identify an issue or opportunity around which you feel frustrated and disempowered—an issue that if acted upon, would positively impact you and your team. What actions can you take to be more empowered in this area?
2. What barriers will you confront?
3. Who can support you and how?
4. What is your first step?
5. By what date will you have taken this first step?
6. Who can hold you accountable?
7. How will you know if you have been successful?

Wrap-Up

Being empowered is good for you and your team. Unfortunately, however, unless you are on a SuperTeam, few resources in your organization are dedicated to training—either for you or the team leader who has the greatest impact on empowering you. Identify what empowerment looks like for you, and take the initiative to make it happen!

Up Next

One of the greatest ways to learn and become empowered is by asking your fellow team members for feedback and support. In the next chapter, we will discuss the most effective strategies for delivering constructive feedback to your team members.

CHAPTER 6

Supportive Feedback

> Every human being is entitled to courtesy and consideration. Constructive criticism is not only to be expected but sought.
>
> —*Margaret Chase Smith*

Overview

In our youth, we received lots of feedback from our parents, teachers, coaches, and other influential figures, such as grandparents and religious instructors. Some of the feedback was positive, and some was critical, but hopefully all was given in support of helping us grow and develop. Unfortunately, as we enter the workforce, the likelihood of receiving such constructive feedback diminishes dramatically.

On most teams, team members rarely provide one another with feedback, which is viewed as the sole responsibility of the team leader. Unfortunately, most team leaders, quite frankly, are terrible when it comes to giving constructive feedback. In fact, their feedback is more likely to lead to frustration and resentment than improvement. And, the dreaded annual performance review process is at best inert.

In this chapter, you will learn:

- How good your team is at providing supportive feedback
- The critical role of supportive feedback to team member development
- How to show respect when giving and receiving feedback
- Specific tips to improve your ability to give constructive feedback

As a starting point, take a moment to reflect on the following questions.

SUPERSTARTER QUESTIONS

1. When was the last time that you received constructive feedback from your team leader, and did you find it helpful?
2. When was the last time that you received constructive feedback from a team member, and did you find it helpful?
3. Why do you think people in general have such an aversion to providing others with feedback?
4. What should you do to deliver feedback in as powerful a way as possible?
5. If team members regularly offered one another constructive feedback, how would that benefit your team?

SUPPORTIVE FEEDBACK TEAM ASSESSMENT

Instructions: Read each statement below, and, using the following scale, decide how accurately it describes your team:

Strongly disagree: 0 points
Disagree: 1 point
Agree: 2 points
Strongly agree: 3 points

Place the point value of your answer choice on the blank line at the beginning of each of the following statements:

_____ 1. **The team leader provides team members with constructive feedback in a supportive, respectful, and timely manner.**

_____ 2. **Team members provide one another with constructive feedback in a supportive, respectful, and timely manner.**

_____ 3. **Team members ask one another for feedback on their performance.**

_____ 4. **Team members are open to receiving feedback from one another; they do not become defensive.**

_____ 5. **The team leader welcomes constructive feedback from team members.**

_____ **Total score**

INTERPRETING YOUR SCORES

0 to 5: Team members are provided with little to no feedback, or the feedback they do receive is intended to be purely punitive. In such an environment people become highly defensive, and they may even seek to hide their mistakes or shortcomings for fear of being reprimanded. Individual growth and development are stifled. The team leader likely provides feedback only at performance review time, which we all know is largely worthless. Should you find yourself in the position of wanting feedback, we recommend that you take the initiative and request it—whether you will get any is up in the air.

6 to 10: Feedback is likely intermittent, and it is typically given only when a mistake has been made and someone needs to be held accountable. When feedback is given, it is likely vague and not particularly helpful. For example, "You really should have done a better job with that report." Feedback is viewed as going in one direction; it is not a collaborative conversation. There may also be a lack of consistency with who regularly gets feedback and how supportive that feedback is. Team members with close relationships may offer one another straight and constructive feedback, but doing so outside of their in-group would be highly unlikely.

11 to 15: Your team has a culture in which team members welcome feedback and request it from others because they understand its value and ability to make them better. Team members understand that not giving feedback would actually be disrespectful. Team members and the team leader are skilled at giving practical, effective, and concrete guidance. Teams can achieve SuperTeam status only when all players serve as coaches to one another.

ASSESSMENT REFLECTION EXERCISE

Regardless of where your team scored, there is likely an opportunity to become even more effective in this very critical skill. For example, even for teams who rank in the highest category, there are likely some team members more skilled than others at providing quality feedback. Or some team members may be more open to receiving such feedback and willing to act on it. As always, we want you to take the initiative for your own development and the development of your fellow team members.

Identify a recent situation in which you feel that you could have performed better or could have produced a more desirable outcome. Go to a team member with knowledge of this situation, and ask him to give you feedback. For example, "Last week when I gave the presentation to our team, I felt that I wasn't clear and I rambled. I'd appreciate your thoughts on how I could have done a better job." Make sure to take notes, and thank him for his advice. Also, consider looking outside your team to those with whom you regularly interact—for example, someone in another department, a customer, or even a vendor—and request feedback on an issue relevant to that relationship.

Supportive Feedback Defined

Giving supportive feedback is a form of coaching, and the term refers to the sharing of perceptions, opinions, and advice in a straightforward and constructive manner for the purpose of helping another person improve. Feedback, no matter how critical in nature, is always to be given in the spirit of caring about your team member's growth, development, and success. Effective feedback is encouraging, specific, and actionable.

We typically view giving feedback as the responsibility of the team leader. However, it is in fact the responsibility of all team members. In SuperTeams, individuals are just as likely to initiate giving feedback as they are to request it; by the way, this includes the team leader.

The Critical Role of Supportive Feedback

Most of us are woefully unaware of our deficiencies. We think we are better, smarter, funnier, and harder working in comparison to others than we often are. Imagine, for example, asking your team members to score how hard they work compared to the rest of the team on a 1-to-10 scale. In theory, the scores should average out to 5. This never happens; the average always comes out as significantly higher.

It is not necessarily a bad thing to think positively of ourselves—it certainly beats the alternative. It is just that our skewed self-assessment reduces our perceived need for improvement. We consistently see clear evidence of this phenomenon when people undergo a 360-degree assessment. This tendency to overestimate our good qualities also explains why it is nearly impossible to create a valid self-assessment tool to measure engagement. The essential quality of engagement is a willingness to give high levels of discretionary effort. If you ask people the extent to which they regularly go above and beyond, they dramatically overestimate.

Respect and Supportive Feedback

As we discussed earlier, there is a strong correlation between the extent to which people are respected and their ability to influence others. We listen to, value, and act on feedback provided by those we respect.

During a feedback conversation, the person giving the feedback must show respect to her team member. The recipient of the feedback shows respect by actively listening, remaining open to the feedback, being willing to act upon the advice, and being appreciative that his team member cared enough to help him.

Feedback Culture

Team culture is perhaps nowhere more important than in the area of team members giving one another constructive feedback. How successful people are in navigating the world of telling others they aren't perfect depends largely on the extent to which there is a "safe" environment. Team members must trust that feedback is given in the spirit of support and that it is not in an attempt to harm them in some way. Without a foundation of trust and respect, you can forget about team members providing one another with any sort of critical feedback. The risk is just too great.

You can help to build and reinforce a feedback culture by regularly providing and requesting feedback from your team members. The more respected you are, the more you serve as a role model to your fellow team members. When a highly respected team member asks for feedback—especially from more junior team members—he sends the message that everyone's opinion matters and that peer coaching is an important part of team culture.

Why We Avoid Giving Supportive Feedback

If you haven't noticed, most of us dogmatically avoid providing others—including our friends and family members—with critical feedback. We fear offending people and hurting their feelings, and we also fear that it will increase the likelihood that others will be critical of us. In truth, allowing team members to perform at a suboptimal level shows disrespect to both the individuals and the team.

People actually get offended when their team members are not straight with them regarding their poor performance. Wouldn't you want to know if your team members felt as though you were underperforming and they had feedback that would help you improve? If you care about your team members and about your team being successful, you will take the initiative to provide constructive feedback in a supportive manner.

Coaching Is a Skill

Being an effective coach requires many skills. Of course, the good news is that skills can be taught and acquired. The many tips that follow will, we hope, put you on that path of becoming a powerful coach to your team members. (We focus here on the coaching skill of providing "constructive feedback" to address performance problems. Obviously, an essential part of being an effective coach is providing positive feedback as covered in Chapter 4.)

SuperTips for Giving Feedback

1. Ask permission. Before launching into giving feedback, ask permission. For example, "I'd like to give you some feedback on the presentation you gave yesterday. Would that be OK?" Asking permission demonstrates respect for your team member. It also reduces the likelihood that he will become defensive, and, thus, he will actually "hear" you and be open to the feedback.

2. Pull, don't push. One of the most common and significant mistakes that any coach, team leader, or team member can make is to *tell* the other person what she did wrong and *tell* her how to fix it. This approach tends to elicit two primary thoughts: "No kidding, I screwed up—does he think I'm an idiot?" and "Stop attacking me." And it immediately leads to the person becoming defensive and shutting down. Telling a team member what to do and how to do it rarely leads to that individual fully owning the solution. Effective coaching actively engages others in a discussion of what went wrong and how things could have been done differently. Again, this is a collaborative process that leads the "player" to take ownership of the problem and solution.

3. Focus on behavior. Confine your comments to specific examples of behavior. For example, "I noticed you raising your voice with that last customer." Remain as objective and fact based as possible. Do not make the feedback about the person. For example, you wouldn't want to say, "Wow, you really lost it on that last customer!" And NEVER talk about a person's attitude as in: "You've really got to change that lousy attitude." You should care about changing behaviors, not attitudes. By the way, once you change behaviors, attitudes shift as well.

4. Avoid judging. People don't want to feel as though they are being judged and found guilty by their peers. Avoid preaching and talking down to your colleagues. Instead of saying or communicating in so many words, "You really blew that!" try, "It doesn't look like that went the way you expected it to. Would you like to talk about it?" Start with the assumption that your team member wants to succeed.

5. Be empathic. Constructive feedback is often given when things don't go well, and under such conditions, team members naturally feel vulnerable. Start by demonstrating empathy and understanding. For example, "Looks like that was pretty rough in there." If you can authentically relate to the experience, you might say something like, "Something similar happened to me last year, so I know what it feels like." Isn't this what you'd want someone to say to you?

6. Include what worked well. Avoid using absolute terms such as "always," "never," and "all." Statements built on these terms are often inaccurate and not helpful because they fail to distinguish what worked from what didn't. They also lead to people becoming defensive and focused on invalidating the statement. For example, "That was a terrible presentation" suggests that there was nothing at all redeemable. Did the meeting start on time? Was the information accurate? Were the slides effective? When you acknowledge what worked well, you are viewed as fair, and your constructive feedback is viewed as more credible. Your feedback is also more effective because it is more targeted.

7. Take a TeamWe approach. If the situation is a problem for the individual, then it is a problem for the team. Approach every feedback conversation with the mindset of it being a collaboration. The intention is always to support the individual in such a way that he improves, which, in turn, makes the team stronger and more effective.

8. Seek to understand. Listen. Ask questions. Don't make assumptions. The first goal of any supportive feedback conversation is to fully understand the situation from your team member's perspective. We often don't have all the information and misinterpret behavior. Paul once got really upset during a training session because a participant was "playing" on her iPad. As it turned out, she was taking notes. Instead of immediately jumping to conclusions, use language such as, "It seemed to me," "I noticed," "I'd like to check something out with you," and "Is this a fair representation of what happened?"

9. Speak from the "I" perspective. Speak from the "I" perspective with phrases such as "This is what I observed," "From my perspective," and "Your behavior came across to me as." Yours is only a perspective—treat it as such. By the way, you may want to ask yourself if what you view as problematic behavior is coming from a place of personal bias. Just because someone handles a situation, makes a decision, or completes a task differently from what you would have done, that person's solution is not necessarily wrong.

10. Be straight. Although yours is a perspective and you want to be respectful of the other person's view, don't beat around the bush or water down your feedback. If you do so, you risk the chance of the other person not fully appreciating your concerns or seeing any real reason to change how she is doing things.

11. Describe the behavior's impact. Once you've identified the behavior, focus on its impact on others. For example, "So we agree that for various reasons you've been consistently late to our team meetings. What you may not realize is that others view this behavior as disrespectful; it communicates that either the meeting is not important to you or your time is more important than the time of your team members. Also, when you arrive late, it is disruptive and distracting, and it makes team members feel that they have to repeat themselves for your benefit. At times, we wait for you, and, thus, we start the meeting late. Can you see how your being late has quite a negative impact on the team?" Often, just this conversation can resolve the problem entirely, and if not, it is certainly an appropriate starting point.

12. Be selective. If you believe that there are multiple areas in which feedback should be given, focus the conversation on the one or two issues that you feel are most critical. Otherwise, the person will likely become overwhelmed and feel as though she is being attacked; her experience is, "Where is this all coming from?"

13. Choose the time and place most conducive to a constructive conversation. Be sensitive to where and when to hold the conversation. Although immediately is best, it may not always be the most appropriate. Almost without exception, you want the meeting to occur in private. As soon as the behavior occurs, you might say, "I'd like to chat with you about how things turned out with the last client meeting. When would be a good time to speak?"

14. Prepare. Don't shoot from the hip—especially if you are emotional. Take time to prepare for the conversation. Constructive feedback is most effective when it is delivered in a thoughtful, organized, and calm manner.

15. Focus on going forward. Although your conversation will naturally begin with an understanding of what happened, quickly focus on what needs to be done. Also, use the incident as a learning opportunity so that it may be avoided going forward.

16. Everyone plays. Often, more junior team members do not feel comfortable providing feedback to more senior team members or their team leader. Of course, this isn't how things work on a SuperTeam. Team members with more experience should make it "OK" by asking more junior team members for their feedback. Such behavior reinforces a culture of openness to feedback, continuous improvement, equality, respect, and belief that every team member's opinion matters and adds value.

17. Show you believe. Let the other person know that you believe in his skills and abilities. When team members underperform, they often begin to doubt their abilities and believe that other team members have lost confidence in them. It is critical that people know that their team members believe in and support them.

18. Break it down. In order to come up with the best course of action, spend time thoroughly reviewing what happened and the circumstances surrounding it. The outcome may have been influenced by decisions and events set in motion months earlier. The initial game plan could have been fundamentally flawed. You are much less likely to come up with an effective strategy to address the problem if you don't fully understand what caused it.

19. Come up with a game plan. "Where do we go from here?" "What are our options?" "Are there other team members who can help out in this situation?" "What resources do we need to get the job done?" You want to come up with as specific and actionable a strategy as possible. For example, you might say, "Based on our discussion, it sounds like the best approach would be to request a meeting with the client, apologize for underdelivering, propose how we will make things right, and commit to meeting our obligations going forward. How does that sound to you?" Also, take the time to identify any potential pitfalls and discuss contingencies. The plan should include a specific time to follow up and review the results.

20. Secure the person's commitment. You must make sure that the team member leaves the conversation fully committed to the plan. The best way to accomplish this is to elicit the solution from the team member. For example, "We've talked about a lot of ideas. Where do you think we should go from here?" Make sure to clearly review what was decided, and ask the team member to put into writing the agreed-upon plan—doing so will ensure that everyone is on the same page and is committed to executing the plan.

21. Practice. Anyone who wants to deliver excellent performance spends time practicing. For example, if the decision was made to request a meeting with a disappointed client, you would want to outline that conversation and practice it with another team member realistically playing the part of the client. The education from this practice will lead to a much more effective intervention.

22. End on a positive note. Leave the person feeling positive about the conversation and decisions made. Express your confidence in his dealing with the situation now and in the future. Let him know that you are happy to lend your support whenever he may need it.

Rick was a young, loyal, hard-working, intelligent, and extremely motivated individual who had recently been promoted to department manager. His ascendancy up the corporate ladder seemed certain except for a single fatal flaw, namely, his approach to managing others. His most serious offense centered on providing excessively critical feedback—especially in public. When a team member "screwed up," Rick used it as an opportunity to embarrass the individual so that he could show who was "boss." He felt that since he was young, he had to "flex his muscles" to be taken seriously by the team and gain their respect. How wrong he was.

Obviously, Rick's management style resulted in team members feeling disrespected, embarrassed, and resentful. Performance declined as team members disengaged; they actually wanted the young, arrogant team leader to fail. Much to his credit, the CEO recognized the situation and began mentoring Rick directly. Using the RESPECT Model as a framework, the CEO helped Rick to understand that respect, and subsequently power, comes only when team members feel respected. Thanks to the coaching of his CEO, Rick became extremely skilled at providing his team members with constructive feedback and ultimately earned their respect.

On Your Playing Field

Select one area in which you could benefit from getting feedback and advice. If you're not sure what area this might be, begin by asking others on your team. You may also want to speak with your team leader and review your last performance review.

Select three team members, at least one more junior and one that you do not know well, and ask to meet with them. Share that you are looking to improve in a particular area and would like to get their perspective on your performance and suggestions on how to improve. It is that simple! It is also unbelievably powerful.

Wrap-Up

Sadly, our family, friends, and coworkers often withhold giving us constructive feedback that could make us better people and better team members—and, of course, so do we. We hold back because we fear hurting others' feelings or having them retaliate in some way against us. In order for a team to be a SuperTeam, the team members must fully embrace the fact that giving and receiving feedback are the respectful things to do and the only ways for the team to be as effective as possible.

Some people believe that asking for feedback makes them appear weak. In reality, the opposite is true: doing so demonstrates strength, confidence, and a commitment to self-improvement. Effective peer coaching is a critical element of a SuperTeam culture. Is it part of your culture?

Up Next

In this chapter we discussed the strategy of providing other departments and individuals with feedback in order to increase interdepartment collaboration. In the next chapter we continue to discuss the critical role that collaboration and partnering play in a team's exceeding their goals and objectives.

CHAPTER 7

Partnering

> The greater the loyalty of a group toward the group,
> the greater is the motivation among the members to
> achieve the goals of the group, and the greater the
> probability that the group will achieve its goals.
>
> *—Rensis Likert*

Overview

Partnering generally refers to two or more people collaborating, most commonly to achieve a common goal. However, partnering in the context of SuperTeams goes beyond simple collaboration. Individuals in partnership work together in an ongoing committed relationship in which each has the other's best interests at heart. Partnerships work best when everyone wins.

Anyone who has ever been in a long-term relationship can attest to both the power and the challenges associated with partnership. It can be tough enough for a team of two to function effectively, let alone the typical business unit with 10, 20, or more members, all of whom have unique experiences, perspectives, and personalities. SuperTeams figure out how to navigate through the challenges and develop team members who act as committed partners to one another.

In this chapter, you will learn:

- Why partnering matters
- How effective your team is at partnering

- How to be a better partner with other teams and departments in your organization
- Different types of partnerships
- 20 keys to effective partnering
- How to create a strategy for improving partnering within your team

As a starting point, take a moment to reflect on the following questions.

SUPERSTARTER QUESTIONS

- How would you define a successful partnership?
- Think about a partnership that became dysfunctional. What happened?
- Do your team members relate to one another as partners or as coworkers?
- Does the team leader treat team members as partners and collaborators or as subordinates?
- How successful is your team when it comes to creating powerful external partnerships with other departments?

PARTNERING TEAM ASSESSMENT

Instructions: Read each statement below, and, using the following scale, decide how accurately it describes your team:

Strongly disagree: 0 points
Disagree: 1 point
Agree: 2 points
Strongly agree: 3 points

Place the point value of your answer choice on the blank line at the beginning of each of the following statements:

_____ 1. **Team members actively support and have one another's best interests at heart.**

_____ 2. **Team members value achieving team goals over individual accomplishments and personal agendas.**

_____ 3. **Team members are willing to compromise and make sacrifices for the sake of the team.**

_____ 4. **Team members and the team leader collaborate to achieve the team's goals.**

_____ 5. **Our team avoids working in silos and effectively partners with others inside and outside of our organization.**

_____ **Total score**

INTERPRETING YOUR SCORES

0 to 5: Yours is a highly dysfunctional team with highly frustrated team members—many of whom play for TeamMe. Team members view one another more as competitors than as collaborators, and they are concerned with what is best for them. This dysfunction makes effective partnerships outside the team impossible. It may actually be in the best interest of the organization to either disband the team or identify a team leader extremely skilled in dealing with conflict and building a cohesive team.

5 to 10: There are likely cliques in your team. Within each clique there is mutual support, harmony, and respect. Individual loyalty and commitment is greater to these subteams than to the team as a whole. There may be power struggles between the cliques for resources and influence. The team leader may himself be more closely aligned with a particular clique; regardless, the team leader is ineffective in breaking down the barriers between the subgroups to create a single unified team.

11 to 15: As in any partnership, team members bring their own unique personalities, perspectives, and differences of opinion. SuperTeams are characterized by team members who have a strong mutual respect for one another and are willing to sacrifice and compromise for the benefit of one another and the team. If you achieved a score at this level, team members not only partner successfully with one another, but they are also likely to do so with the team leader, sponsor, other departments, and their customers.

ASSESSMENT REFLECTION EXERCISE

As you reflect on your answers, what stands out? Where is the greatest opportunity for you and your team to partner more effectively? We find that one of the greatest opportunities exists in teams partnering with other departments. Try the following exercise—it could make a significant difference in team and organizational functioning:

1. Name the teams and departments with which your team regularly interacts.
2. Which of these relationships is most significant and could benefit the most from improved relations? (It could be as simple as needing to communicate more effectively.)
3. At your next team meeting, initiate a conversation about being a more effective partner with this other group and the benefits that would be realized.
4. Ask for permission from the group and team leader to take the initiative and contact the team leader of the other group and have a conversation on this topic. Ask others if they would like to participate. (Depending on your organization, it might be necessary to include the team leader.)
5. During the meeting, express your interest in being a better business partner. Ask permission to join one of their team meetings for the purpose of eliciting feedback on how your team could be more helpful. Leave with as many specific suggestions as possible.
6. Share these suggestions at your next team meeting, and discuss how best to address them and who will take on working on what tasks.
7. Ask the other team to appoint a liaison with whom you can regularly communicate.

We promise that if you engage in this kind of partnering within your organization, yours will be perceived as a SuperTeam!

Partnership Types

There are all kinds of partnerships in life. In the workplace, you may find yourself in multiple partnerships—some formal and some informal. Some are intended to accomplish very specific tasks, and others may serve as ongoing sources of support. For example, mentoring and coaching relationships can be viewed as partnerships that may last a few months or years. Your team may be in partnership with other teams within and outside the organization, including most prominently your customers.

Many organizations form strategic partnerships. In general, all partnerships are formed with the idea that the unit can accomplish more than the individual entity alone. Or tasks can be accomplished at a higher level of quality, more efficiently, or more economically. Intended to be beneficial and mutually satisfying experiences, partnerships all too often fail to reach their potential and end poorly. Of course, the question is, why?

20 Keys to Effective Partnering

As you might imagine, during the course of our research we identified many factors necessary for creating effective partnerships within teams. At the risk of being a bit corny, it just so happens that the most critical factors all happened to begin with the letter C, and, thus, we present the "C list of 20 factors" that we believe makes for "A partnerships."

1. Clear and compelling vision. Team members cannot fully partner if they are not energized by and fully committed to a clearly defined vision. When team members don't find the vision compelling, they are much less likely to fully engage and provide maximum effort. If you don't believe in your team's vision and you have other opportunities, we recommend looking into them. Team members must share the same clearly articulated vision, or they risk misalignment of goals and efforts.

2. Core values. What are the core values of your team? What are your core values? Have you ever written them down? If not, we suggest that you take the time to do so. Core values guide your decisions and behaviors. They determine what is important to you. Core values also guide the behaviors, decisions, and culture of a team. If values aren't aligned, neither will anything else be. Do your core values differ significantly from those of your team members? For example, TeamMe and TeamWe players represent two very different sets of core values.

3. Culture. Whether you realize it or not, all teams have a culture. Culture matters because it drives the behavior of team members; it leads to the social mores of the group and an understanding of how things work. In the Introduction, we mentioned Edward Deutsch who established the "No Jerk Rule" in his law firm. His organization is driven by a culture of respect. When people—including senior partners—act in ways that violate that culture, they no longer have a place at the firm. How would you describe your team's culture? Do all team members fit into the established culture? Do you? Partnering and collaborating are greatly diminished when people don't believe in and support the same culture. Whenever you bring in new team members, make sure they fit into the culture from the start.

4. Clarity regarding roles and responsibilities. Effective partnering requires each team member to clearly understand the other team members' roles and responsibilities. What do you count on your team members for, and what do they count on you for? You would be surprised how often team members *assume* they know the answer to this question and are wrong. Have you ever been on a team when someone said, "I thought *you* were going to do that?!" Important tasks drop through the cracks when people make assumptions. The roles and responsibilities of each team member should be clearly documented from the beginning. A good starting point is obviously a job description, but we all know that responsibilities—and even roles—morph over time. We recommend that all team members and the team leader "check in" to avoid inaccurate expectations. If you don't believe that your current job description matches your responsibilities, we recommend that you have a conversation with your team leader and the human resources department.

5. Complementary roles and synergy. Although it is not always the case, in most teams different team members bring unique skills and abilities to the relationship. While there may be some overlap, these talents often complement one another, and, thus, the collective is capable of accomplishing more together than apart. When teams and partnerships are formed, the people involved must be clear as to the talent needed to accomplish the vision and mission. If that talent does not exist within the team, the members must have the resources available to hire or contract individuals who have such skills, and they must be in agreement to do so.

6. Cross-training. One of the biggest weaknesses of teams is the lack of cross-training among members. In fact, teams can come to a screeching halt when a team member is out for an extended period or exits the team with little notice. In powerful partnerships at least one team member is trained to accomplish at least the core responsibilities of each role so that people can support and cover for one another. Would the functioning of your team greatly suffer if one team member were to exit suddenly? If so, is it possible for some team members to acquire knowledge and skills in one another's key areas of responsibility?

7. Competence. Obviously, partners count on one another to be competent in their roles and to fulfill their part of the bargain in terms of their responsibilities. Unfortunately, this is not always the case. Have you ever been on a team and found that another person just didn't have the skills to get the job done? It may well not be his fault. Individuals are often put into positions without the requisite skills to succeed. Partnering is demonstrated when team members take responsibility for helping others to learn the skills or, if possible, to shift their responsibilities to take advantage of their strengths.

8. Clear performance goals and expectations. Setting clear performance goals and expectations is closely related to setting clear roles and responsibilities. However, they are different in significant ways. To clarify, a partner may have the role of the technical director and all the responsibilities associated with the technical needs of the department. The specific expectations and performance goals for this individual get into another level of specificity. Teams and partnerships get into trouble when people say things like, "OK, so you just take care of this part." Different partners may well have different interpretations of what "taking care of" one's part looks like. It is critical that people's performance can be clearly evaluated and everyone knows the criteria by which success will be judged. (This is also critical for appropriate compensation that we will touch upon shortly.) If team members' performance goals are not clearly defined, we suggest doing so as soon as you finish this book.

9. Commitment. Whenever people form or join a team, they invariably express their commitment to one another and to fulfilling their responsibilities to the best of their abilities. Unfortunately, we all know that for lots of reasons, commitment can wane, and, as commitment goes, so does the functioning of the team. Partners stay committed to one another over time, and when issues arise that risk diminishing that commitment, they are willing to have direct and honest conversations to address the issue. If commitment is lessening on your team—either with you or another team member—have the courage to initiate such a discussion. (Make sure to stay focused on your observations of behavior, and as always, hold this conversation in a respectful manner!)

10. Collaboration. By definition, partnering involves active collaboration, which is at the heart of any SuperTeam and an ingrained part of the culture. Many teams are composed of groups of people acting as individuals focused on accomplishing specific tasks in isolation. (Think assembly line.) If they do collaborate, it is by design and out of necessity to accomplish a specific objective—furthering the relationship is not important. Such a way of working completely misses the value of being on a team. In contrast, SuperTeams are composed of TeamWe players in partnership committed to supporting and learning from one another and to figuring out ways to make the team more successful.

11. Character. Have you ever been on a team where someone lacks integrity? Nothing kills the possibility of partnering more than a team member who acts irresponsibly, immorally, and dishonestly. Having integrity also means keeping one's word. Integrity is everything when it comes to building partnerships based on respect and trust. There's not much more to say than yours will never be a SuperTeam with even one such member.

12. Communication. Do we need to say more? Communication is the lifeblood of any relationship. When blood stops flowing, death ensues. As we said earlier, whenever disrespect enters a relationship, communication leaves. Communication is most important when there is trouble in a relationship, and when there is trouble in the relationship, most people stop talking. Being partners means being willing to have the tough conversations. If you have partners with whom communication has dwindled for whatever reason, take responsibility for opening up some lines of communication, and get the blood flowing again.

13. Compromise. When it comes to having long-term healthy partnerships, the ability to compromise may be the most important of all. This may be hard to believe, but you are not always right—yours is not always the best way. And, this may be tough to swallow, even if you are *right*, but if continually battling for your position means beating up your partners until they cave in, you may be winning battles but losing the war. If you respect your team members, don't treat them and their ideas disrespectfully. In SuperTeams, partners listen to one another, and winning means finding the solution that best serves the customers.

14. Checking in. Teamwork and effective partnering often falter because people fail to regularly check in with one another by simply asking some version of, "How is this working for you?" We propose holding what we call a *relationship review*. At least once a quarter, team members should formally meet and discuss how well the team is functioning on an interpersonal level. Are people getting what they need from one another to be successful? Are some team members struggling, and do they need more help? Have there been any breakdowns in communication? Are there any issues that need to be discussed such as individual roles and responsibilities? The idea is to bring up any issues that might inhibit collaboration. If frictions have developed between individual team members, they need to take responsibility to clean things up for the sake of the team. If neither is willing to take the initiative, then another team member or the team leader should step in and make that conversation happen. Does all of this sound like fantasy to you—completely impractical? Guess what? This is exactly how team members operate in a SuperTeam.

(Obviously, we encourage people to bring up issues as soon as they occur. The quarterly relationship review meeting simply ensures it happens in a structured and comprehensive manner.)

15. Constructive feedback. Most people hate giving constructive feedback about as much as they hate hearing it. However, providing your partners with feedback to help them improve is absolutely critical for them and the team. As discussed in the previous chapter, your constructive feedback should always come from a place of wanting to help the other person be successful. Give feedback in such a way that the other person can really hear you without becoming defensive. If you are on the receiving end of getting constructive feedback, you may also want to elicit feedback from other team members on the issues.

16. Conflict management. A significant relationship killer is the inability to deal effectively with conflict situations. When people hear the word *conflict*, they often think of confrontation, and they shy away. As we just discussed, people shy away from giving critical feedback because they fear that it will result in a conflict situation. But it doesn't have to go that way. We encourage you to reframe your thinking from confrontation to collaboration. Almost without exception, and quite naturally, conflict enters partnerships. In fact, a lack of conflict might actually be a bad sign because it could mean that people are not expressing their concerns. Handled correctly, conflict can be very healthy, and it can lead to stronger relationships and wiser decisions. Avoiding conflict or dealing with it poorly is sure to impede partnering.

17. Change management. Stuff happens, and teams must evolve, adapt, and grow in order to accommodate changes—for example, technology, competition, or customer demands—both internal and external to their organization. If they don't adapt, the teams will become irrelevant in their attempt to stand still. In the words of the great W. Edwards Deming: "It is not necessary to change. Survival is not mandatory." SuperTeams are particularly skilled in dealing with change for nearly all the reasons cited in this chapter.

18. Consequences. Team members need to be held accountable when they fail to fulfill their commitments. Period. Having clearly defined roles, responsibilities, and expectations and regularly checking in with one another can greatly reduce the likelihood that people fail to live up to expectations. However, people do drop the ball—we all do—and this often occurs because well-intended team members underestimate what it will take to complete the task, or the circumstances change. In a SuperTeam, team members make one another aware of potential problems as soon as they become aware of them. Their fellow team members partner with them to see how they can help out. This may include literally helping accomplish the task, securing additional resources, offering advice, or helping to create a revised plan. Without question, the individual assumes full responsibility and does not place the blame elsewhere. Good partners come up with solutions, not excuses. If the person continues to underdeliver, various consequences may become appropriate including changes in roles, responsibilities, autonomy, decision-making responsibilities, and financial compensation.

19. Compensation. Although SuperTeam members play for TeamWe, everyone wants and deserves to be recognized and rewarded appropriately for their contributions. When people contribute equally but are compensated disproportionately, this violates what is known as *equity theory,* and, naturally, those undercompensated become upset and disengage. A real challenge is when individuals' roles and responsibilities change over time and compensation is not adjusted accordingly. Clear strategies and criteria should exist to deal with this issue.

20. Courage. Being a good partner means being courageous at times—for example, speaking up when doing so would rock the boat or when you know that your opinions will be met with great resistance. You may well need the courage to trust others. You may need the courage to stand up to someone more senior and experienced, or even to your team leader. Sadly, there are countless examples of egregious medical errors committed by doctors in front of other medical staff who did not have the courage to speak up. Thankfully, there has been concerted effort by those in the medical profession to create patient care teams in which all caregivers work in partnership and are empowered to say: "STOP!" Lives are saved when team members become courageous. Although your team may not be making life and death decisions, there are still critical moments in which a decision—or lack of decision—could dramatically alter your team's ability to complete your mission. Do you have the courage to stand up to the rest of your team when you know it is the right thing to do?

Courage is what it takes to stand up and speak; courage is also what it takes to sit down and listen.

—Winston Churchill

On Your Playing Field

While thinking about your team, review each of the 20 Cs, and identify those that you believe are the strengths for your team and those you believe are the weaknesses. What areas represent the greatest opportunities to increase a sense of team members truly being in partnership with one another? Is there one factor that adversely impacts several other factors—for example, poor communication?

Identify just one area that you believe, if improved, would have the biggest positive impact on your team:

1. What would improvement look like in this area? How would team members act and behave differently from how they are doing so now?
2. If there were improvement in this area, what would be the benefit to the team?
3. Can you identify any reasons that caused this to be a problem area so that you may know better how to address it? (For example, perhaps there was a conflict situation that was never resolved.)
4. What would it take to turn this weakness into a strength—or at least get it back to neutral? Who needs to be involved? What resources are required? Would training help?
5. Bring the issue up at a team meeting, and state your concerns. Ask if others would be willing to join you in addressing this issue.

6. Create a plan, and present it to your team members and leader. Ask for feedback and the help you need to make your plan successful.
7. What is the first step in this plan (if you know it)?
8. By when will you complete this first step?
9. What criteria will you use to judge whether your plan has been successful?

Wrap-Up

We hope that you can *see* (yes, bad pun intended) that in order to maximize a team's effectiveness, team members must form powerful partnerships with one another and with those external to the team. And there are lots of challenges to doing so! SuperTeams exist in a partnership culture in which team members are committed not only to the mission of the team but also to one another and to external partners. Is this the culture of your team?

In organizations, real power and energy are generated through relationships. The patterns of relationships and the capacities to form them are more important than tasks, functions, roles, and positions.

—*Margaret Wheatley*

Up Next

What are you expecting next? Because that is the topic we will be addressing! We will discuss the importance of setting clear expectations and holding yourself and your team members accountable to achieving them.

CHAPTER 8 Expectations

> If you expect nothing from anybody, you're never disappointed.
>
> —*Sylvia Path*

Overview

Have you ever had a boss or significant other who assumed that you had special mind-reading powers? The most common reason that people fail to live up to our expectations is that they simply do not know what the expectations are in the first place. We assume that people know what we expect of them, or they believe that they know what we expect from them, or they don't know and are too embarrassed to admit it. SuperTeam members know what is expected of themselves and each other and admit it when they don't.

In this chapter, you will learn:

- The critical role that setting clear expectations and priorities plays in team member performance and goal attainment
- Your team's strengths and weaknesses when it comes to establishing clearly defined expectations and holding people accountable
- How to hold an *expectation calibration exercise*
- A strategy to improve expectation setting on your team

As a starting point, take a moment to reflect on the following questions.

SUPERSTARTER QUESTIONS

1. When have you failed to meet another's expectations due to a misunderstanding or miscommunication?
2. What does your team leader expect from you?
3. What do team members expect from one another?
4. What is the impact of poorly communicated expectations?
5. What is the impact when team members are not held accountable for achieving their goals?

EXPECTATIONS TEAM ASSESSMENT

Instructions: Read each statement below, and, using the following scale, decide how accurately it describes your team:

Strongly disagree: 0 points
Disagree: 1 point
Agree: 2 points
Strongly agree: 3 points

Place the point value of your answer choice on the blank line at the beginning of each of the following statements:

_____ 1. **Team goals and objectives are clearly defined.**
_____ 2. **Team members are given clear and consistent direction regarding work priorities.**
_____ 3. **There are clear team rules, procedures, guidelines, and governance.**
_____ 4. **Team member roles and responsibilities are clearly defined.**
_____ 5. **Team members are held accountable for achieving their individual goals.**

_____ **Total score**

INTERPRETING YOUR SCORES

0 to 5: Team members are confused, frustrated, and lost. They do not know where to invest their energies and, thus, tend to be halfhearted about their work. Team members may be working at odds with one another and certainly cannot benefit from any synergy. As a whole, the team is both inefficient and ineffective. There is little likelihood that the team achieves its goals and delivers on the expectations of its customers. Team members should approach their team leader and insist on clarity around individual and team goals and objectives. If he is unable to do so, you may have to consider going to his manager. Your team simply cannot function in this environment.

6 to 10: Scores in this range indicate average performance in each area or a distribution of some low and some high scores. Having clearly defined goals and work priorities tends to receive the lowest scores. All too often the team leader believes that he is providing both clear expectations and consistent direction when in fact he is coming across as ambiguous and confusing. Team members may feel that they have to figure out what their team leader wants, and they become extremely frustrated when work priorities suddenly shift. Often the team leader simply isn't aware that her team needs more direction. Poor communication is often at the root of the problem, which can be easily corrected by team members taking initiative to let their team leader know that they need more direction—don't assume that she can read your mind!

11 to 15: Your team members know what is expected of them and can move confidently toward their goals. Efficiency is not lost by people standing around trying to figure out what to do or working at odds with one another. People know the rules and policies, and they follow them. Collaboration and synergy are greatly enhanced under such circumstances. Moreover, team members take responsibility to successfully complete their objectives and hold one another accountable when this doesn't happen. It is only when team members achieve their individual and collective goals that they have a chance of exceeding their customers' expectations and, thus, achieving SuperTeam status.

ASSESSMENT REFLECTION EXERCISE

Suggest to your team leader and team members that they hold an *expectation calibration exercise*. Individual team members write down what they believe is expected of them in a prioritized order. They can also write down what percentage of their time they spend in each activity. The team leader should do the same. Team members should read through one another's write-ups. They should identify instances in which there is a mismatch in how they believed a team member was or should be spending her time. Call a group meeting and discuss. Resolve any differences in perceptions. This exercise will allow for much greater clarification and synergy among team members and the team leader.

Underpromise and Overdeliver

One of the most frequent errors made by individuals and teams is making overly ambitious promises to one another and their customers. We do this because we want to look good. Or we may feel as though we are being forced to say "yes" because of the boss's or the customers' expectations. If, in fact, you achieve your goal, you have simply met expectations—obviously, this is positive, but it does not qualify as SuperTeam results. Consider the benefit of slightly lowering and then exceeding expectations.

For example, if a customer requests a report within the next 24 hours, you would likely be better served to set the expectation that it will be completed within the next three days. When you deliver it sooner, you will look great in your customer's eyes. Obviously, urgent circumstances require immediate attention. Or if you know the task will only take a few minutes, do it as soon as you get the request, and you will exceed the customer's expectations.

Now, we are not suggesting that you dramatically lowball your customer, team members, or team leader—they likely have some idea of how long the task should take. For example, if you were asked to create a report that typically takes 30 minutes, it would be foolish to give an estimate of two weeks—you would look unresponsive if not incompetent. Try to find a middle ground, keeping in mind that tasks often take longer than you estimate and that if you fail to meet agreed-upon expectations, you will come off looking less competent than you would like.

By the way, all of this applies also to your internal customers who may be depending on you to accomplish your tasks so that they may accomplish theirs. I am sure that we have all been frustrated waiting for others to complete tasks we are relying on. So make sure that you fully understand the requested task, how your success will be judged, what resources are available to you, and what barriers you might confront. Then, figure out a realistic goal and give yourself some cushion and the opportunity to impress your customer.

A most wonderful example regarding the impact of poorly communicating expectations comes from the television comedy series *Seinfeld*. In the episode titled "The Bottle Deposit" (number 131, May 2, 1996), the character George is following his boss Mr. Wilhelm down a corridor when Mr. Wilhelm begins telling George that he needs him to do something, at which point, he walks into the bathroom. George stands outside the door in a panic trying to decide whether to follow him. He eventually decides to go in just as Mr. Wilhelm—who assumed that George had been listening the entire time—exits from the bathroom stall. Mr. Wilhelm tells George that this assignment is a top priority and walks out. Of course, George has missed all the details of the assignment. He explains the situation to his friend Jerry and asks for his advice:

George: *Well, I still don't know what I'm supposed to do. I don't even know what my assignment is.*

Jerry: *Ask him to repeat it. Tell him there was an echo in there.*

George: *I can't. He's been on my case about not paying attention. Besides, it's too late. I already told him I heard him.*

Jerry: *You know what you do? Ask him a follow-up question. Tell him you're having trouble getting started, and you want his advice.*

George: *Yeah, follow-up question, that'll work.*

The next day George goes to work and jumps up as Mr. Wilhelm walks by his office:

George: *Uh, Mr. Wilhelm.*

Wilhelm: *Yes George.*

George: *Hi, I was just uh . . . , I just had one little question about uh, my assignment.*

Wilhelm: *Yes, well, I trust things are moving smoothly. Mr. Steinbrenner's counting on you, you know.*

George: *Yes, Yes. Very smooth, supersmooth. No, but I really wanna attack this thing, you know. Sink my teeth into it. So I was just wondering . . . , what do you think would be the very best way to get started?*

Wilhelm (appearing confused): *Get started? I don't understand, George.*

George: *Well, I was wondering . . .*

Wilhelm: *You mean you haven't been to payroll?*

George: *Payroll? No, no, I haven't done that.*

Wilhelm: *Well, what's the problem? Now come on George. I told the big man you were moving on this. Now, don't let him down!*

George continues to be frustrated throughout the episode trying to figure out what his boss wants. In the end, Mr. Wilhelm tells George that he is delighted with his work. George, of course, has no idea what he did or how he did it. Of course, it usually doesn't turn out this way!

Setting Expectations in the Real World

Although we aren't able to provide as humorous an example as *Seinfeld*, let's look at a real-world situation with real-world implications.

Steve was a dedicated, loyal, technically skilled, and hard-working employee in a medium-sized construction company. Over the course of five years, he had moved his way up from foreman, to supervisor, and to manager, and he was viewed as someone with the potential to find himself in one of the big offices.

One thing held him back—namely, his inability to set clear expectations and hold his team members accountable for achieving them. Steve was extremely concerned about being liked, and, thus, he welcomed any opportunity to give positive feedback. He was a great cheerleader, but he wasn't an effective coach. His fear of holding people accountable was holding his team back—at both the individual and overall team level. He regularly made exceptions and excuses—especially for those with whom he had a relationship outside of work. His inequitable treatment of others and inconsistent application of the rules led both subordinates and superiors to lose respect for him and to lose faith in him that he could be successful in his current role, let alone a more senior leadership position.

The worst thing that can happen to a player [from a player's perspective] is for him not to know what the coach is really thinking about him.

—*Bill Parcells, Coach, New York Giants*

Steve's failure to set clear expectations significantly contributed to his inability to hold people accountable. It is a lot easier to let people get away with poor performance when you make the criteria for success vague. Steve *assumed* that his people knew what was expected of them. His lack of clarity resulted in confusion and frustration, especially when team members were informed that they had missed the mark. Poor performers hung on far too long and detracted from the team's ability to be effective. Instead of helping team members to correct course, he allowed them to stray further and further until his boss had to intervene and direct Steve to terminate the employee. This is not the situation you want if you're looking to advance your career. By the way, would it surprise you to know that Steve's boss had failed him in exactly the same way?

In the context of the RESPECT Model, Steve showed disrespect for his team members and organization by not adhering to company policies and procedures, by holding employees to different standards of performance, by failing to provide constructive and critical feedback that team members needed to improve, by not setting clear expectations, and by failing to hold people accountable. He failed to do his job as a manager and coach, and, as a result, his team and the organization suffered. If your primary concern is to be friends with and liked by your coworkers, avoid taking on a supervisory position.

If setting clear expectations and holding people accountable are areas where you struggle, there is good news. These are very teachable skills, and the following steps will help you improve immediately. If you already *know* each of these steps, are you consistently applying them?

1. Ensure that all team members are clear regarding the mission of the team; all expectations should be driven by the mission.
2. Identify the specific tasks necessary to accomplish the mission.
3. Make sure that team members understand the importance of each task and their role in completing it.
4. For each task, set specific goals that include the following criteria: quality of the work, quantity of the work, resources available, and time frame. Team members must be clear regarding each of these expectations.
5. Break down goals into smaller units so that it is easier to reach those marks and easier to make course corrections.
6. Ensure that you have players with the right experience and skills. If you don't, either provide training or provide some form of external support.
7. Make sure that team members know the priorities. (Frequent shifts in work priorities kill team member morale and productivity, and they should be avoided at all costs.)
8. Set clear parameters in terms of autonomy and decision-making authority. Team members need to know the boundaries.
9. Have team members provide regular updates on progress— ideally in a morning huddle meeting.
10. Hold a more comprehensive weekly or biweekly team meeting in which the progress of each task is reviewed, obstacles are identified, and solutions generated.
11. Most important, team members must be held accountable for achieving their objectives. Always start by making sure that the individual understands the expectations, knows why they are important, and has the required skills. The individual should receive coaching and support, but if she continues to fail, her poor performance should be met with appropriate consequences—for example, verbal or written reprimand, reassignment, or reduction in responsibilities, decision-making authority, autonomy, or compensation, or, ultimately, termination.

On Your Playing Field

Identify one area in which you or other team members are failing because of unclear expectations and apply the steps above. If you are not the team leader, get support from him and other team members.

Make sure to discuss the impact that this lack of clarity is having on team functioning and effectiveness; you need to impress people with the importance of setting clear goals and objectives. Once agreed upon, make sure that they are written down and distributed to avoid further confusion. Poor communication often contributes to misunderstanding, so pay attention to keeping the lines of communication open.

Wrap-Up

We hope this book is living up to your expectations, and we certainly apologize if that is not the case. Although the information in this chapter may have come across as applying primarily to the team leader, that is not the intention.

We want to leave you with the clear expectation that every team member is responsible for understanding what is expected of him or her and for committing to and delivering on those expectations. Team members should never commit to achieving goals that they do not believe they can meet. Moreover, team members must be willing to take responsibility for holding one another accountable—this is often the difference between a good team and a SuperTeam.

Up Next

Of all the RESPECT drivers, consideration—or more often, the lack thereof—may have the greatest potential to impact an individual's experience of being respected. In fact, lack of consideration by the team leader or other team members frequently underlies a person's decision to leave a team. We will tackle this very important issue in the following chapter.

CHAPTER 9 Consideration

> People do not care how much you know until they
> know how much you care.
>
> —*John Maxwell*

Overview

It is actually quite astonishing how inconsiderate team members are to one another, although, sadly, it is probably a reflection of society. When people are treated inconsiderately, they feel disrespected, and they become angry, hurt, disappointed, and disengaged. In contrast, when team members treat one another with consideration, it demonstrates that they care for one another as human beings—over and above their working relationships. When people feel as though others are concerned about them and their welfare they feel respected, and they engage. Simple stuff isn't it?

In this chapter, you will learn:

- The extent to which consideration is a part of your team's culture
- Why consideration matters
- The critical role of empathy
- Specific tips for increasing consideration on your team

As a starting point, take a moment to reflect on the following questions.

SUPERSTARTER QUESTIONS

1. The idea of treating others with consideration is clearly quite simple, and most would agree, it's the right thing to do. Why then do you think that people don't act more thoughtfully toward one another?
2. Do your team members care about one another on a personal level?
3. Would you consider your team leader thoughtful? Why?
4. Have you ever been treated without consideration by a team member or leader? If so, what was the impact on you?
5. What are the most powerful ways to show consideration for team members?

CONSIDERATION TEAM ASSESSMENT

Instructions: Read each statement below, and, using the following scale, decide how accurately it describes your team:

Strongly disagree: 0 points
Disagree: 1 point
Agree: 2 points
Strongly agree: 3 points

Place the point value of your answer choice on the blank line at the beginning of each of the following statements:

_____ 1. **Team members care about one another on a personal level and demonstrate kindness and consideration toward each other.**

_____ 2. **Before decisions are made, the impact on team members is considered, and those affected are consulted.**

_____ 3. **The team leader demonstrates appropriate compassion when team members have personal problems.**

_____ 4.   **Team members and the team leader respond quickly to one another's communications and requests.**

_____ 5.   **Team members actively elicit and respect one another's thoughts and opinions.**

_____   **Total score**

INTERPRETING YOUR SCORES

0 to 5: You'd better have thick skin to be a part of your team and not take things personally. If you have personal problems, leave them at home—your team members and leader don't care. You can also keep your opinions to yourself. Just put your head down, and do what the boss says. If you like warm and fuzzy, this isn't the team for you.

6 to 10: It is likely that some people are considerate and thoughtful and others are not. In which category would your team members put you? Team members are probably not actively and intentionally discourteous to one another. They just aren't thoughtful. Average scores also often come from teams on which people do not regularly interact with one another. In these cases, team members need a structured way to stay connected with one another.

11 to 15: Team members and the team leader are thoughtful and care about one another's well-being. They actively support one another on both a personal and professional level. People's opinions matter, and team members are consulted on decisions before they are made. Morale is likely high, and your team has little turnover. Your team's culture of treating one another with consideration spills over into interactions with internal and external customers, as well as vendors.

ASSESSMENT REFLECTION EXERCISE

Like respect, an individual's perception of how considerately he treats others can differ significantly from the perceptions of his coworkers. Do you have team members wearing such blinders? The following may sound incredibly basic, but we promise that it is also quite powerful. If the goal is to make someone more considerate, then this is how you do it:

1. Identify an individual whom you would like to see be more thoughtful. Find a way to be considerate to her. It could be very simple. For example, offer to buy her a cup of coffee, volunteer to help her out on a task which she dislikes, compliment her work, or ask about her children. In other words, model thoughtfulness.
2. Ask her to do something very simple that would demonstrate consideration, and then let her know how much you appreciate it. She has likely had few experiences in which she actually received thanks for doing something thoughtful. Although likely unconscious, she will find the experience reinforcing and be more likely to comply with requests going forward.
3. Repeat both steps. Once you get the ball rolling, you will build on the momentum.

John did his job, but he didn't really pay much attention to other team members and their needs. When he did interact, it was strictly for business purposes. He tended to be quite negative, and he never offered to lend a hand. He walked past his team members without a greeting, and he would never bother to wish people a good weekend or ask about their weekend on Monday. If a team member was sick, John wouldn't think of telling him that he hoped he felt better. He often didn't even bother saying, "Thank you." John wasn't a bad guy, and he wasn't mean or vindictive. He simply wasn't thoughtful.

John was a loner who did his own thing and simply wasn't interested in connecting with his coworkers. His team members viewed him as rude and not a team player. He was on the outside, and his team members had little interest in getting to know him or in collaborating with him. One day, a fellow team member, Marge, realized that this was a bit of a vicious circle: John did not treat others with consideration, and in return people didn't bother being considerate toward him. She also realized that this was not healthy for the team because it made them less cohesive. So she decided to take responsibility for bringing John more into the fold. She started with the assumption that John was not a bad guy, but just largely unaware of his impact on others. Her goal was to influence his behavior in such a way that he experienced consideration and was reinforced for showing consideration to others.

John and Marge worked in the accounting department, and she knew that John became particularly stressed at the end of the month, especially around some data entry issues. Instead of just saying, "Can I give you a hand?" to which he probably would have said "No," she said, "John, I've got some free time, and I'd like to give you a hand with the data entry." (Although it may appear minor, making an offer of specific help increases the likelihood of its being accepted.) John was clearly grateful for the help, and he did end up thanking Marge. A few days later Marge asked John for a simple favor: to look over a short presentation that she had put together and give his feedback. Her request demonstrated her respect for John's opinion, and he readily agreed. John offered a few suggestions, and Marge sincerely thanked him.

On the following Monday, Marge swung by John's cubicle and asked how his weekend was. She appropriately probed and found out that his son, Sam, was on a traveling baseball team, and they had spent the weekend out of state in a tournament. She also found out that John had a younger child, a daughter named Samantha. John had rarely experienced a team member being interested in his life. Although John didn't ask about Marge's weekend, she volunteered that she and her husband had seen a really good movie, and they had enjoyed dining at a recently opened restaurant. She left by saying she hoped he had a good day. Understand, John simply wasn't used to such interactions.

The next day at a team meeting, Marge agreed to take the lead on a new project. After the meeting, she asked John if he would be willing to take on a small role, to which he agreed. She thanked him and suggested that they grab a cup of coffee to discuss the project. Before jumping into business, Marge asked John how his son's baseball team was doing. So she and John began to connect and collaborate. Something else happened: other team members began to notice their interactions, and because Marge was highly respected, they decided that John must not be such a bad guy. They began being more friendly toward him. Over time John experienced more and more positive reinforcement from team members, and he began actually offering his help and regularly saying, "Good morning" and "Thank you." Was John destined to be dubbed "Mr. Thoughtful" on the team? No, but his lack of consideration was no longer an issue, and he was clearly part of the team.

Consideration Matters

If you don't believe that showing people consideration and thoughtfulness matters, we're here to tell you that it does. Just because you might not need it doesn't mean that your team members don't. Yes, people do differ in how important it is to them, but always err on the side of too much rather than too little. Even when people say they don't care, they often do. You don't often hear people say, "Oh, that Johnny, he is just way too considerate. He should really be a little more selfish and less thoughtful."

The greatest opportunities to show consideration typically revolve around personal crises—especially when it comes to someone's health or the health of a family member. Of course, being able to show consideration in these areas requires that team members be willing to open up and share what is going on. Unfortunately, when an individual is labeled as inconsiderate, her fellow team members will make little effort to get to know her on a personal level. Thus, opportunities to provide support when it is most needed are lost because the team members simply aren't aware of what that individual is going through.

We could write a book composed entirely of stories of how poorly team members and team leaders treat one another. One of Paul's favorite stories is the supervisor who wrote up a team member for an unexcused absence when she went into labor during her shift. You can't make this stuff up. In another more mundane example, a woman had to undergo an operation and was out of work for two weeks. Not a single person on her team or the team leader bothered to send flowers or a card. In another case, a gentleman had knee replacement surgery and was out for three weeks. He told only his supervisor who didn't bother telling the rest of the team until people started asking where the recuperating team member was. The human resources manager didn't know for a week, and she sat across the hall from him.

Empathy

On the list of the most critical qualities to have as a human being, empathy ranks near the top. Being able to put yourself in others' shoes and thoughtfully respond to them will earn the appreciation of everyone you ever meet. Unfortunately, empathy is very hard to teach. We would like you to consider the following: nearly everyone in your organization is dealing with heavy personal "stuff," which, quite frankly, is a whole lot more important to them than their work.

You have no idea of the extraordinarily difficult situations—including aging parents, rocky relationships, financial difficulties, and teenagers who are driving them crazy—that some of your team members are confronting. Paul was once delivering a training program, and during a break a woman came up and said, "I really want to apologize for being so tired and yawning. I was up all night with my husband who is a paranoid schizophrenic." Give each other a break.

When Bill Parcells was coach of the New York Giants football team, he once asked a rookie player to stop by his office.

When he showed up, Parcells said, "Tell me about yourself."

"Well, I played special teams and . . ."

"No," Parcells interrupted, "I mean tell me about yourself. I know about your football."

SuperTips for Being Considerate

1. Do I know you? Perhaps the most basic way to show consideration and thoughtfulness is simply getting to know someone on a personal level. Take the time to get to know the people you work with and to learn what is important to them.

2. Knock. Don't barge into people's offices. Knock and ask permission to enter. If they are on the phone or have someone else in the office, return later.

3. Be considerate of others' time. If you want to speak with a team member, don't just barge into his office and assume that he has been standing around all day waiting for you to walk in. Ask if he has a moment to see you or if you could schedule a good time to meet with him. Obviously, always be on time for meetings, which, unfortunately, is rarely the culture in most organizations.

4. Be careful using ASAP. Don't dump work on others and tell them that you need it right away. Give people advance notice and ample time to get their work done. Consider asking when they might be able to get it to you.

5. Respect others' lunch breaks. Don't bother people with business issues when they are eating lunch or on some other break.

6. Be interested in others' weekend activities. Authentically ask people and be interested in what they are doing over the weekend. Getting this specific information allows you to actually ask about it on Monday, instead of the old "How was your weekend?" "Good, how was yours?" If you asked the questions before the weekend, then the question and exchange after the fact actually becomes meaningful and not simply obligatory.

7. Offer your help. Offer to lend your support to others, especially around specific tasks.

8. Be supportive. Acknowledge and support people when they've had a bad day. For example, "Paul, sorry to hear that deal didn't work out. You'll get 'em next time."

9. Help the newbies. Make sure that new hires get shown the ropes. Think about what it was like when you first joined the organization. Did people take you under their wing, or were you left to survive on your own? Let new team members know that you are going to help them get adjusted and you are happy to answer any questions they may have.

10. Understand the needs of introverts. Introverts need time to process information. If you know that you're dealing with an introvert, don't make that person come up with an answer on the spot. Don't force him to agree to something without allowing him the time to fully consider the options and his decision.

11. Listen. Demonstrate your interest in your team members' ideas and especially their concerns. Show others that what is important to them is also important to you. Ask questions to fully understand their concerns. If you're the kind of person who loves giving advice, realize that sometimes people just want to feel heard.

12. Find out what is important to others. Ask your fellow team members what is important to them. Would they like to learn different skills at work or take on different responsibilities? Do they have skills that they aren't using and would like to? What is important to them outside of work?

13. Be empathic. Always look for opportunities to be empathic. Let others know that you care about what they are going through and you are there to help. For example, if you find out that a team member is dealing with, say, a health issue or crisis in her family, buy her a simple card and let her know that you are thinking about her.

14. Don't ask. Just do. Often when we see a person struggling with something, we ask, "Can I help you?" The person usually responds with something like, "Thanks, but I'm fine." If the nature of the help the person needs is obvious, just jump in and start helping.

15. Smile. As simple as this sounds, smiling makes other people feel good. Always frowning and being negative adversely impacts the mood of others.

16. Make coffee runs. If you're running to Starbucks to get a cup of coffee, ask a coworker if she would like to join you or if you can bring something back.

17. Shhh! Is there anything more annoying than someone having a lengthy personal phone call loud enough for everyone around to hear? If you're going to be on a personal call, find a personal place to make that call.

18. Be flexible. Look for opportunities where a more flexible work schedule would make a real difference for someone. For example, there are many single parents responsible for dropping their children off and picking them up from school or daycare. And, obviously, there are those days when children are sick and must stay home. If you're in this situation, you know how stressful it can be. If not, please put yourself in the shoes of the parents. Teams should support their team members in creating a flexible work schedule that may, if possible, involve working some hours from home.

19. Plan for your absences. If you are knowingly going to miss work, please be responsible to make sure that your work is covered and coworkers who may be affected are aware of your absence and whom they may report to for assistance.

20. Anticipate others' needs. And take care of them before they even ask. We perceive such proactive behaviors as particularly considerate because it shows without question that the others are thinking about them.

21. Give your undivided attention to others. When you are having a conversation, look at the other person—not your phone or computer!

On Your Playing Field

When team members treat one another with genuine consideration, they create a highly cohesive team. Team members appreciate one another on a personal level and understand what is important to each person. Nearly all of us could do better at showing consideration—especially to those we may not know particularly well. Try the following exercise and make yours a more considerate team:

1. Identify the three people that you know least well on your team. (If you have a small team or know everyone extremely well, select business colleagues from other departments or even your customers.)
2. Write down your responses to the following:
   a. What is the name of each individual's spouse or partner?
   b. What are the names of this person's children?
   c. Does this person have pets? What kinds?
   d. What does this person like to do outside of work?
   e. What else is important to this person?

   If you do not know the answers to these questions, make it a goal to get this information over the next month.

3. Going forward, use this information naturally during informal conversations or to show that you are thinking about them. For example, "Did you play softball this weekend?" "Did Johnny leave for college yet?" "How are things with the new puppy?"

Wrap-Up

The RESPECT Model is about taking action to show others respect. In the area of consideration, start with the Golden Rule: treat others as you would want to be treated. Realize that it is quite easy to show consideration toward those with whom you already have good relations.

The opportunity to make a difference on your team is to show consideration to those with whom you might not have the best of relationships. Like building respect and trust, if you want to increase consideration on your team, you need to take the initiative.

Up Next

If you've been playing along, you'll know that we have only one letter left in our acronym: T. And we bet you can guess what it stands for. Like respect, trust is absolutely fundamental to any good relationship, and it is essential to the creation of a SuperTeam. Enjoy finding out about trust in a team environment and how to increase it on your team.

CHAPTER 10

Trust

> Set your expectations high; find men and women
> whose integrity and values you respect; get their
> agreement on a course of action; and give them
> your ultimate trust.
>
> —*John Akers*

Overview

As is true of respect, relationships work only when people trust one another. When we distrust others, we feel unsafe and become guarded; we become suspicious of others' intentions, and we keep our distance. Communication and collaboration break down. Unquestionable trust among team members is a core characteristic of SuperTeams.

In this chapter, you will learn:

- The level of trust that team members have for one another
- The impact of trust and distrust on team functioning
- The relationship between trust and respect
- How respect makes teams more efficient and effective
- Specific strategies for building trust with your team members

As a starting point, take a moment to reflect on the following questions.

SUPERSTARTER QUESTIONS

1. Is there anyone on your team whom you don't trust? Why?
2. What is the impact on a team when people don't trust one another?
3. Think of someone for whom you have lost trust. What happened?
4. How can you gain someone's trust?
5. How can you build greater trust within your team?

TRUST TEAM ASSESSMENT

Instructions: Read each statement below, and, using the following scale, decide how accurately it describes your team:

Strongly disagree: 0 points
Disagree: 1 point
Agree: 2 points
Strongly agree: 3 points

Place the point value of your answer choice on the blank line at the beginning of each of the following statements:

_____ 1. **Team members and the team leader keep their promises and commitments to each other.**

_____ 2. **When issues and concerns arise, team members speak to one another and not about one another.**

_____ 3. **Team members can be counted on to have one another's back.**

_____ 4. **Team members feel safe offering their honest opinions to one another and the team leader.**

_____ 5. **The team leader demonstrates confidence in team members' skills and abilities.**

_____ **Total score**

INTERPRETING YOUR SCORES

0 to 5: Watch your words and your back. If you have one or two people on your team in whom you can trust and confide, consider yourself lucky. Gossip is rampant and toxic. Team members are suspicious of one another's motives, and in such an environment there is little communication or collaboration. Yours is a "gotcha" culture where the game is about catching others screwing up and pointing the finger at them. The best strategy—other than moving to another team—would be to keep your head down and mouth shut.

6 to 10: There are likely cliques in which people trust one another inside but not outside their group. There are probably a few people who do a lot of gossiping and in the process reinforce distrust, which distracts people from doing their work. Gossip is a real productivity killer. Team members do not feel that they can be entirely open with one another, and communication is limited. People are naturally concerned more with their own success than that of others. If possible, we suggest trying to stay outside of any subgroup by showing respect to everyone and allegiance to the mission of the team rather than to individuals.

11 to 15: With trust comes great freedom—freedom in that team members don't have to worry about gossip or being thrown under a bus by another team member. Team members assume the best intentions from their colleagues. They actively collaborate and communicate without fear that they will somehow be taken advantage of. High levels of trust among team members and with the team leader is absolutely critical in order to be a SuperTeam.

ASSESSMENT REFLECTION EXERCISE

To what extent is trust either contributing to or distracting from the effectiveness of your team? Are there people whom you do not fully trust on your team? What is it about them that you don't trust? Is it personal or technical? If you do not feel as though you can trust their technical skills, how can you help them get the support they need to be more effective? If the loss of trust is associated with an interpersonal issue, have the courage to initiate an authentic conversation to resolve the issue for the sake of team functioning.

Trust and Respect

Trust and respect go hand-in-hand. Like respect, we can trust people on both technical and interpersonal levels. In most cases, when we don't trust a person, we also don't respect that person. When trust is broken, respect walks out the door, and we suggest that you walk out the door as well.

Restoring trust is theoretically possible, but it rarely occurs.

Recognize that there can be such a thing as being too trusting, in which case people become vulnerable to being taken advantage of. Others need to earn your trust just as you earn theirs.

Trust = Freedom

When team members trust one another, they are able to interact with one another with great freedom. Team members do not feel constrained in offering their opinions for fear that they will be judged harshly by their colleagues. They freely share information with one another and trust one another to do their jobs. They work collaboratively without any concern that a fellow team member will take credit for their contributions.

Trust is absolutely essential for team members to be able to provide critical feedback to one another. In the words of Patrick Lencioni, author of *The Five Dysfunctions of a Team*, "Trust is knowing that when a team member does push you, they're doing it because they care about the team." When people trust one another, they can have straight conversations and get to the point without worrying about the other person becoming defensive. Do your team members trust one another enough to provide this kind of feedback? SuperTeam team members do.

Gossip Kills Trust

If you could make only one rule on your team, it should be that team members talk to one another, not about one another. It is the respectful and mature way to handle situations involving interpersonal conflict with a fellow team member. If you want to know the litmus test for gossip, here it is: **If you wouldn't say it in front of the person, it is gossip.**

If gossip is at all a problem on your team, we implore you to enact this rule. And hold one another accountable. If a team member comes to you and begins to gossip, handle it like this: "STOP! Our team agreed that if we had a problem with someone, we would speak directly to that person. That is my request."

Sad but true, almost immediately after a workshop in which we recommend the "No Gossip Rule," participants start gossiping about how certain team members really need to take this class! Can you imagine someone on your team doing so? Paul once worked with a client where an employee would regularly go into his manager's office and rant about how stupid the CEO was. Paul's advice? The next time he comes in to complain, ask him to hang on, call the CEO, put him on speakerphone, and let him know that you have an employee in your office who would like to share some concerns. Problem resolved.

Team cooperation increases commensurate with increases in trust.
—*Mike Krzyzewski, Coach, Duke University*

Trust Leads to Efficiency and Effectiveness

This may sound odd, but the more trust there is in a relationship, the less need there is to communicate. Why? Because when you say you are going to do something, I actually trust that you are going to do it, and I don't have to worry about checking in and checking up on you. If you need something, you'll reach out; otherwise, I know you've got it. When you say or do something, I take it at face value, and I don't have to worry about any underlying personal agenda. Our relationship is not a chess match in which I have to carefully decide my next move.

When I don't trust you to do your job, my own decisions are impacted and may become compromised. For example, consider any team sport in which players pass one another a ball. Passes are often made when the intended receiver isn't even looking—the person passing trusts that his teammate will turn in time to make the play, and the receiver trusts that when he turns, that the ball will be there. That is what trust looks like on the playing field!

Trust is the glue of life. It's the most essential ingredient in effective communication. It's the foundational principle that holds all relationships.

—*Stephen Covey*

SuperTips for Building Trust

1. Overcommunicate. The more you communicate, the more transparent you appear, and the more people trust that you aren't holding anything back. If you want to build distrust, withhold information and appear secretive and selective in what you communicate.

2. Give trust. Just like respect, if you want to get trust, you've got to give it. When you show that you trust others, they are much more likely to believe that they can trust you.

3. Ask for feedback. As we've discussed, asking your team members for feedback shows that you respect their opinions and wish to improve. The opportunity to build trust lies in how you respond to the feedback. If you openly accept the feedback and avoid becoming defensive, you show your team members that you can be trusted to receive such feedback—they don't have to worry about biting their tongue.

4. Disclose. Especially when you are new to a team or you get a new team member, take the time to get to know others and to let them know you on a personal level. The more we know about people, the more we feel that we can trust them.

5. Count on me. Again, when it comes to new relationships, let your new team members know what they can count on you for.

Let them know that you trust them to do their job and that you'll lend them a hand when they need it.

6. I don't know. When you don't know something, admit it. Doing so lets other people trust that you won't take responsibility for an assignment for which you aren't qualified. Also, admitting a weakness shows vulnerability and demonstrates that you trust your team members not to use it to their advantage or your disadvantage.

7. I blew it. Similar to admitting when you don't know something, taking ownership for your mistakes makes you vulnerable and lets your team members know that you will not try to cover up your mistakes, make excuses, or redirect blame.

8. Follow through. To state the obvious, do what you say you're going to. Don't make promises you can't keep. It is better to underpromise and overdeliver.

9. Act with integrity. Be honest and forthright in all dealings. Always speak the truth, and do the honorable thing. Stand up for what you believe in.

10. Walk your talk. Never say one thing and do another; never be hypocritical.

11. Listen. Actively listen to others. Paraphrase, and use reflexive listening skills such as saying, "Let me make sure I understand what you're saying." In addition to showing respect, it allows others to trust that you heard and understand their views.

12. Make sacrifices. Take one for the team. Help out another team member even if it means that you'll have to give up some of your resources—for example, time that you'd be using to complete your own projects.

13. Be consistent. Be consistent in your word and work. Doing so lets your team members know that you are reliable—a critical part of being trusted.

14. Use common sense. You've got to prove to others that they can trust your judgment. For example, don't make a decision based on a rule or policy that makes no sense in a particular situation. Unfortunately, some people don't have much common sense, which then becomes a real handicap in establishing trust.

15. Give others a fair shake. Give your team members the benefit of the doubt and the opportunity to prove themselves.

Be willing to compromise, and always give credit where credit is due.

16. Be brutally honest. The people we trust most in life—that is, our best friends and, hopefully, family—are also those who can give us the most sensitive feedback. For example, "You've got bad breath." When people are willing to provide us with such feedback, our trust in them increases significantly.

17. Clean up. Distrust is driven by specific behaviors and incidents. Rebuilding trust is extremely difficult, and the further away you get in time from the incident, the more difficult it becomes. If you want to save the relationship, you must initiate a conversation with your team member and address the issue head on and as soon as possible after it occurs.

On Your Playing Field

As always, the real value of this book comes when you apply our behavioral tips to your relationships. Try the following:

1. Identify a team member with whom you have an opportunity to build greater trust. Do you believe that the person fully trusts you? Why or why not?
2. What would be the impact on the team if your level of trust increased?
3. Was there a specific incident that decreased trust in the relationship?
4. Assume responsibility for increasing respect in the relationship. Choose three SuperTips, and apply them to this relationship.
5. How will you know if there is an increase in trust?

Wrap-Up

If your team members don't have a great deal of trust in one another and in their team leader, you don't have a shot at being a SuperTeam. Trust is built up over time, and it can be lost in the blink of an eye. Trust is something to be nurtured over time, and we hope that the tips offered in this chapter will help you do that.

If you've acted in a way that may have led others to distrust you, immediately take responsibility for doing what you can to make it right. You owe it to your team.

Up Next

Well, we trust if you've read this far that you are getting value out of this book, and for that we are grateful. Congratulations, you've graduated to Part III. The next section will be dedicated to building and leading a SuperTeam.

Assembling a SuperTeam

Coming together is a beginning.
Keeping together is progress.
Working together is success.
                    —*Henry Ford*

In Part II, we described the factors that impact directly on team member engagement—how the RESPECT Model explains why individuals give the maximum possible discretionary performance.

In Part III, we build on this and conventional team wisdom to show how to assemble SuperTeams. We explore how the RESPECT Model, when applied to different types of teams and to every stage of their recruitment, deployment, and even disbanding, elevates team performance beyond the sum of the individual contributions to those teams.

Never doubt that a small group of thoughtful, committed people can change the world. Indeed, it is the only thing that ever has.

—Margaret Mead

CHAPTER 11

Understanding Team Types

> One reason—perhaps the major one—for these near failures [large corporate] is the all-but-universal belief among executives that there is just one kind of team.
>
> —*Peter F. Drucker*

Overview

Throughout our lives, we have seen many different types of teams and what these teams needed to be successful has varied. But we have realized the relevance of the RESPECT Model to them all.

In this chapter, we look at the different characteristics of teams that we have identified in the course of our research, and we look at how all of us (team members and team leaders) can apply the RESPECT Model to turn our own team into a SuperTeam.

SUPERSTARTER QUESTIONS

Check which of the following types of teams you belong to:

TEAM FOCUS AND PURPOSE

_____ **Leadership teams.** The role of a leadership team is to look ahead, cope with uncertainty and ambiguity, make the best possible judgments (often with inadequate data), and then develop and communicate the vision, mission, and strategy for an organization, region, function, or unit; to resource it; and to inspire the organization itself to succeed.

_____ **Management teams.** Management teams (which may also be leadership teams—more about that later) take the vision, mission, strategy, and values of the organization and use them, for their respective parts of the organization, to develop and oversee the implementation of plans to deliver. They ensure the right things happen right.

_____ **Operational teams.** Operational teams implement those plans and produce things—for example, manufacturing, sales, marketing, or logistics. In other words, they do things.

_____ **Problem-solving teams.** Problem-solving teams investigate issues and develop solutions. For example, they make quality or process improvements, address compliance issues, and fix system bugs.

TEAM SIZE

_____ Very small team (5 or fewer)
_____ Small team (6 to 20)
_____ Large team (21 to 100)
_____ Very large team (over 101)

TEAM COMPOSITION

_____ Mixed skills
_____ Specialists—in other words, largely single skills or skill types; for example, football teams, engineering teams, or computer programming teams

PROXIMITY OF TEAM MEMBERS

_____ Largely **colocated** when working together
_____ Largely **virtual** when working together

TEAM DIVERSITY

_____ Homogeneous: common background, culture, values, and so on
_____ Diverse

TEAM ASSESSMENT

Instructions: Read each statement below, and, using the following scale, decide how accurately it describes your team:

Strongly disagree: 0 points
Disagree: 1 point
Agree: 2 points
Strongly agree: 3 points

Place the point value of your answer choice on the blank line at the beginning of each of the following statements:

_____ 1. **The purpose and focus of our team is absolutely clear.**

_____ 2. **We are the right size to be efficient yet effective.**

_____ 3. **We have the mix of skills needed to handle the work of the team and to work well together.**

_____ 4. **We are appropriately located, and we have easy working access to each other.**

_____ 5. **We are suitably diverse, and we capitalize on that diversity in how we work.**

_____ **Total score**

INTERPRETING YOUR SCORES

0 to 5: Your team appears to be poorly formed, and it may well struggle to meet its goals. Unless you score high on question 1, the team appears to lack clarity around its purpose. This may well be part of the reason that it is ill resourced and poorly equipped. Before looking at adding or removing resources and capability, make sure that the real reason for the team is clear. Then revisit the resources and the position of those to meets its goals.

6 to 10: Your team appears to be reasonably clear about its goals and appropriately resourced to meet them. However, there are clearly some weak spots. Make sure that the purpose of the team is 100 percent clear and understood. Then look at refining the capability, and make sure that you can make the best use of the talent you have. Finally, you may need to revisit the team size.

11 to 15: Your team appears to be set up for success—with clear purpose, correct structure, and the composition needed to succeed. You still have some opportunity to refine the team, but it has the potential to be a SuperTeam.

ASSESSMENT REFLECTION EXERCISE

The team with the best players does not always win. The critical issue is to understand the type of team that you need and then to build that team with the right resources, in the right place, to achieve their goals.

Think about each of the team types that you have identified for yourself. How do you think the team type impacts the number and types of team members you need? How does the team type impact how the team should be structured and how it should operate? How does the team type impact the style of team leadership it needs?

The Significance of Team Types

Teams, or tribes as they were originally called, have existed for thousands of years. From the earliest days of human existence, we quickly learned that some things are achieved more easily or better, or perhaps they can be achieved **only**, by combining the capabilities and efforts of a number of people. However, not all teams are equal. Building the Pyramids demanded a quite different type of team from the one needed to crack the genetic code or to win the Masters Tournament in the United States.

Decades of study and experience led to the conventional wisdom that effective teams need the following:

- Clear and shared team goals
- Singular team leadership
- A defined team structure with clear team roles
- Agreed-upon team processes and rules
- Quality communications

However, even with all our accumulated wisdom, teams that should succeed still fail or struggle.

The Walt Disney Company had a difficult time when it first opened its theme park near Paris in 1992. It was a significant operational task due to the park's "cast members" of thousands.

In the U.S. Disney parks, belonging to a team with extremely clear *expectations* and being provided with what was viewed as *supportive feedback* (to keep smiling all day—"You are a cast member in a play, and that is what the script demands") was considered the norm. Not so in France, where employees were not used to being told what to do. The Paris cast members did not view providing service as a positive experience, and they certainly did not accept that being told to "smile all day" was even remotely acceptable. The Paris park team struggled to succeed.

The French team members did not like being "one of the cast," and they sought far more *empowerment* and *consideration*. They also expected to get far more *recognition*, even when they didn't smile! Understanding the team's culture (but not necessarily bowing to it) is key to knowing how to turn a team into a SuperTeam. Disney persevered, stuck to its principles, invested (along with some private investors) in more effective recruitment and selection, onboarding training, and management of individual performance. It eventually succeeded in making a profit in July 1995.

People don't come together only because they need to; they also come together to achieve things because they want to. Choirs, dance troupes, golf clubs, and cycling groups are all examples of this. But does this mutual interest and a shared desire to succeed guarantee optimum success? Apparently not. Churches are closing by the hour. Most parent-teacher organizations struggle to retain active members, and many mutual-interest clubs degenerate as the "inner clique" starts to make the other members feel like outsiders. The same effect occurs in business, yet many organizations still seem to believe that buy-in is the magic ingredient, and they interpret buy-in and commitment to be exemplified by voluntary team membership. The increase in use of voluntary "focus groups," "brown bag lunches," quality circles, and other such teams has been explosive. But the desire by team members to be there cannot compensate for lack of clarity of purpose, having the right skills, and so on. It merely provides the source of energy and commitment.

With all the millennia of practice and decades of experience in our working in teams, wouldn't you expect us to have refined how to make the different types of teams excel into an art form by now? No way.

It would appear that even with clear and shared team goals, singular team leadership, a defined team structure with clear team roles, agreed-upon team processes and rules, and quality communications, teams can and do still fail.

So is achieving SuperTeam status merely as simple as applying the RESPECT Model to teams that have at least met the conventionally agreed-upon standards? Probably not! The real challenge is identifying **how** to apply the RESPECT Model. We firmly believe that the RESPECT Model enables us to achieve SuperTeam status. But each different team type appears to require a different balance of the RESPECT drivers—just as every patient seeing a doctor needs a different combination of treatments. During our research, it became clear that the analysis of the teams that fail produces much clearer evidence of what is happening than the analysis of the teams that succeed. The diagnosis of why teams fail is really quite simple. Most fail because the people on the team simply can't or don't work effectively together.

Teams Based on Purpose or Focus

Team type matters because the different types of teams place different demands on the relationships between the people on the teams and because the people who make up teams bring different perspectives. These two factors combine to create a cocktail of pressures and demands that cannot be, or are not always, met.

In our research, we identified a number of characteristics of teams that appear to influence the most appropriate ways in which to apply the RESPECT Model, and so achieve SuperTeam standards.

Leadership Teams

Leadership teams are charged with creating a vision and bringing the future alive. They have to inspire larger groups to follow their lead and to commit to achieving common goals. They have to enable and resource other teams to deliver. And leadership teams, because they are creating the vision and setting the direction, often need to cope with ambiguity, challenge, and responsibility. Internally to leadership teams, mutual *respect* and *trust* are critically important. Most leadership teams that fail do so because of political intrigue and selfish and/or disrespectful behavior.

Partnering in the face of adversity and challenges and demonstrating collective responsibility can emanate only from a foundation of mutual *respect* and *trust*.

Management Teams

Management teams are charged with creating and implementing plans and making things happen on specification, on budget, and on time. Management teams need to *respect* one another, the organization, and the work they do because their job is to take responsibility for higher-level goals and strategies, work out together how to implement them, and then earn other people's commitment to the plans.

To achieve that, *expectations* and *empowerment* are critically important. Many management teams fail because of a lack of clarity and shared understanding around priorities and roles. Individual managers then pursue their own agendas at the cost of the whole. Worse still, they each manage their subordinate teams in ways that are not aligned with the whole to which theoretically they have bought into . . . mismanagement teams?

The meeting was proving to be a long one. They had started at 8 a.m. with the intention of ending at noon, but it was now 3 p.m. and the caterers were only now clearing away the remnants of lunch. Joshua had gone to the restroom, partly to check his e-mail.

"Hi, Jack. Wow, I thought Tom was never going to stop going on about how we should make his new product and get into that market."

"Yes, me too. He drives me nuts when he gets into one of his I-know-best moods."

"So, why didn't you say anything? We are now going to invest half a million in developing something that will put us head-to-head with the competition where we will probably lose, when we could protect and grow our own niche market for substantially less."

"Well, you didn't say anything, and I didn't want to look stupid by challenging him. My guess is that he had this all tied up before we got here anyway."

Trust within a management team is also critically important—*trust* that you can express your views without others taking your views personally, and *trust* that you can question decisions that do not make sense to you without being viewed as either stupid or aggressive.

Operational Teams

Operational teams implement plans and produce things—for example, manufacturing, sales, marketing, or logistics. In short, they do things.

Within operational teams, it is critically important that *expectations* are clear. If the team leader does not ensure that this is the case, team members must work together to ensure that clarity. Processes like *management by objectives* (MBO) and *goal cascading* have all been deployed by the most highly successful organizations as a means of ensuring this clarity. Many have attempted to push these processes down the organization, much further than management, but with diminishing results. Variations of these business process models—such as the use of *objectives and key results* or OKRs (for example, by Google) and *spider planning*—have also been used. The search for a truly effective paradigm continues.

Within operational teams, clear *empowerment* is also critical. A team can be a SuperTeam only if every individual maximizes his or her contribution. This demands clarity of *expectations*, but even more important, it also requires the authority to act on one's own. "Getting on with it" is a characteristic of all high performers, and SuperTeams are no exception. *Consideration* for individual circumstances helps tremendously.

Operational SuperTeams also provide one another with highly effective *supportive feedback*. This is delivered promptly to maximize the available response time. It is delivered in a noncombative but helpful way, reinforcing a message of "There is no 'I' in 'team.' We are in this together."

Problem-Solving Teams

Problem-solving teams investigate issues and develop solutions. For example, they develop quality or process improvements, they resolve compliance issues, or they fix bugs. Essentially, they fix things that have gone wrong.

The biggest challenge that most problem-solving teams contend with is the opposing forces they face. On the one hand, people want issues fixed, fixed fast, and fixed permanently—"Come on in. You're welcome here. No pressure!" On the other hand, people don't want to be found out!

The expectations of problem-solving teams are usually clear: get to the bottom of the issue; find the cause, not merely the symptom; and fix it! Genuine problem-solving teams need to work like well-oiled machines. So, *partnering* and *consideration* are critically important within the team. All team members need to know that they can proceed with their investigations and can come forward with ideas, and they generally have to have clearly defined authority to act on their findings. But they must also have 100 percent confidence in *partnering* by the rest of the team—no one-upmanship, no stealing ideas, and no posturing. So *supportive feedback* is also key—that is, they need to receive ongoing affirmation or redirection depending on the evidence that is uncovered and the situations that evolve.

Team Size Matters

Yes, it's true: size does matter. Small teams clearly depend for their success on *consideration, partnering*, and *trust*—working tightly together, taking the rough with the smooth, and generally helping one another out. However, as the team size grows, conventional team issues such as structure and processes have to be attended to, merely to ensure that the team can operate.

Establishing effective ways of ensuring clarity of individual *expectations*, providing effective and *supportive feedback*, and ensuring *recognition* for successes are what drives the larger SuperTeams.

Team Composition

Traditional books and training about teamwork stress the importance of having team members with different skills, especially team-working skills. Here, however, we are concerned more with the technical skills people bring to the team. Our research has shown that teams formed exclusively of, for example, engineers or clinicians, behave differently from those teams that have a mix of skills.

Teams with highly mixed skills need clear *empowerment* and *expectations* so that individual members know what both they and their teammates are required to do.

However, in teams composed largely of specialists, too much *empowerment* and *trust* can lead to naive dependency on the specialists. If your team has only specialists, this mutual admiration and support can be immensely powerful. At its best, it creates a level of objectivity and openness that is difficult to replicate; it is far easier to take *supportive feedback* from someone you feel is "one of us" or "on the same page." But, at its worst, a team of specialists can lead to the "old boys club" syndrome: patting one another on the back for even mediocre performance, demonstrating blind trust, and making completely irrational allowances for unacceptable behavior!

SuperTeams of specialists appear to focus on ensuring that they *recognize* their other team members, they *partner* well, and they are *considerate* of others' views and contributions, even those of any nonspecialists who may be part of their team. That is the big challenge—acknowledging any nonspecialists who are often taken for granted.

Proximity of Team Members

Virtual teams experience some significant pressures in terms of communications. In contrast, if teams are colocated, team members find it far easier to see when others are available, seize transient opportunities to speak with one another, observe body language, and get into temporary huddles to review things. What other advantages can you think of from being colocated?

Technology such as videoconferencing, e-mail, and instant messaging all help, but it does not yet resolve many of the issues associated with virtual teams, especially time differences, cultural differences, and even language barriers. These problems have secondary impacts on other factors such as *trust* (it is much easier to develop a trusting relationship with someone you meet physically); *empowerment* (it is much easier, especially emotionally, to give up control to people you can see and connect with easily); and *expectations* (it is far easier to be sure that you have established clarity of shared understanding if you can discuss issues face-to-face, observe responses, and have a fluid exchange of views). Even supportive feedback can be a challenge to deliver over thousands of miles, different languages, and varying time zones—the lack of immediate visual interaction is a serious limitation.

Diversity of Team Members

With globalization, it is difficult, at least in the United States, to find a nondiverse group of people. Yet, despite the massive migrations and ethnic integrations over the last century, we still struggle to understand different cultures and, sometimes, even to acknowledge that they exist. Many corporations still speak of implementing their global values and competencies . . . yeah, right!

On Your Playing Field

Think about the team that accounts for most of your time:

1. What type of team is it (more than one may apply)?
2. Do you have single robust leadership?
3. Do you have clear, shared goals?
4. Do you have the right mix of knowledge and skills on the team?
5. Do you have effective processes for task allocation and management?
6. Do you have effective processes for communication?
7. For optimal performance by your team, select which RESPECT drivers are most important, and note whether each is currently a strength (S) or limitation (L).

RESPECT Driver	Most Important: ✓	Strength (S) or Limitation (L)
Recognition		
Empowerment		
Supportive feedback		
Partnering		
Expectations		
Consideration		
Trust		

Based on the above, what can you do to strengthen RESPECT on your team?

Wrap-Up

All teams need to attend to conventional team-working wisdom and check that they have the following:

- Clear and shared team goals
- Singular team leadership
- A defined structure with clear roles
- Agreed-upon team processes and rules
- Quality communications

Members of true SuperTeams finesse how they work with one another. They consciously focus attention on where they can improve next. SuperTeam performance is a continuous improvement process.

The RESPECT Model and its associated drivers are important in all individual and team environments. Indeed, lack of them provides an explanation for suboptimal performance.

The relative impact of each RESPECT driver is different on various team types based, for example, on (1) why the team exists, (2) the size of the team, (3) the composition of the team, (4) where the team's members are located, and even on (5) the diversity in the team. SuperTeams understand this and take appropriate action to maximize their performance.

Up Next

Every organization does its best to put the most appropriate teams in place (that is, the optimal team types, structures, diversities, and skill mixes). Yet many teams still fail, and when they do, the failure is often blamed not on the team members but on the team leader.

In the next chapter, we explore how to ensure SuperTeam leadership with RESPECT.

CHAPTER 12

Leading the Team with RESPECT

> It is better to lead from behind and to put others in front, especially when you celebrate victory when nice things occur. You take the front line when there is danger. Then people will appreciate your leadership.
>
> —*Nelson Mandela*

Overview

Have you ever noticed how, at the end of the game, every fan of the winning team shouts for joy and jumps up and down, and all of the team members hug one another? Yet, when the team loses, it is usually the captain or the manager, or both, who takes the blame. That is the nature of leadership. Leaders enable teams to succeed. Leaders do not succeed alone.

Even in the highly public world of professional sports, where the skills of each individual player are on display for public scrutiny, where the measures of success are clear and indisputable, where the managers and coaches are changed as frequently as we turn the lights on and off, and where the money is available to pick the absolute best team members, the process still fails. And the same is true in all other walks of life.

Teams with the best set of team players do not always win; they often fail. Consider Enron, a Fortune 500 company employing the best in the world and with an enviable track record—it crashed and burned. Consider the immensely powerful U.S. men's hockey team of 1998, rated equal with Canada for the Olympic gold—only to lose three games out of four and be eliminated by the Czech Republic in the quarterfinals. So great was the shock that some players trashed their rooms in the Olympic Village.

But many teams do excel. Just look at the success of the 1998 Yankees baseball team; England's World Cup Rugby Team of 2003; Margaret Thatcher's U.K. government; Toyota (even despite repeated and highly publicized quality problems); and Apple.

Leadership on a team is *plural*, not singular.

—*Mike Krzyzewski, Coach, Duke University*

A true SuperTeam is a great team with great leadership—that is, they work in perfect synergy. In some cases, the leadership is not all vested in the same individual. Just because you are a team member does not mean that you cannot contribute to the leadership, nor that you are exempt from responsibility for so doing. On many great sports teams, it is the leadership provided by a combination of managers, coaches, and captains that enables those teams to excel.

In this chapter, we explore:

- What makes a great leader
- The differences between leadership and management
- Why leadership matters
- How to lead teams with RESPECT

SUPERSTARTER QUESTIONS

1. Think of a very successful team to which you have belonged or that you have observed. How important was the leader to that team's success, and why?

2. Based on your own experience, what do you look for in a great team leader?
3. What are some of the differences between great team leaders and ineffective team leaders?
4. What differences, if any, do you see between great team leaders and great team managers?
5. Think of a team to which you belong. What leadership value do you add?

TEAM ASSESSMENT

Instructions: Read each statement below, and, using the following scale, decide how accurately it describes your team:

Strongly disagree: 0 points
Disagree: 1 point
Agree: 2 points
Strongly agree: 3 points

Place the point value of your answer choice on the blank line at the beginning of each of the following statements:

_____ **1. The team leader brings the future alive and helps the team understand what true success will look like.**

_____ **2. The team leader enables each team member to understand what really matters and how the team members are going to work together.**

_____ **3. The team leader ensures that each team member knows his or her role, is equipped to fill it, is capable of filling it, and knows how well he or she is doing with respect to it.**

_____ **4. The team leader makes things possible; he or she enables the team to succeed and ensures that the team does.**

_____ **5. The team leader accepts accountability yet shares the credit for the team's successes.**

_____ **Total score**

INTERPRETING YOUR SCORES

0 to 5: If the team is succeeding, it may be despite the leader rather than because of him. There is little direction, and there are probably low levels of commitment. Team members are unlikely to respect the team or the team leader. Teams like this can be successful, but the success is rarely sustainable.

6 to 10: The basics appear to be in place, and you have some leadership taking place. There may be a general sense of direction and some oversight of team performance. There is probably little energy or passion for what the team does.

11 to 15: Your team appears to have effective leadership. The team leader has communicated the team goals, and the team members are probably committed to them. The leadership is in place to achieve SuperTeam status.

ASSESSMENT REFLECTION EXERCISE

We cannot imagine why individuals would join an organization wishing, or even intending, to fail. So, something has to happen when or after they join. Many now argue that individuals join organizations, but they leave their managers or leaders. Leadership is lonely and challenging, and you cannot lead without followers. But you can't make people follow you. Leadership has to be achieved by bringing a positive future alive, sharing it with the team members, enabling them to believe that it is possible, and getting them to commit to making it happen.

1. How effectively is your team being led?
2. How much of the leadership role is being assumed by team members?
3. Is the leadership ensuring that the team is successful?

The Leadership Role

Conventional wisdom tells us that we need the following:

1. Clear and shared team goals. We make sure that these are in place. We put up posters, we remind people at every meeting about the goals, and we routinely post achievements and progress.

2. Singular team leadership. We chair the meetings, we appoint the team, and we make sure that whenever there are differences of opinion, we make the ultimate decision.

3. A defined team structure with clear team roles. We appoint the people, we agree on personal performance plans and objectives, and we conduct one-to-ones on a frequent basis.

4. Agreed-upon team processes and rules. We stick to agreed-upon processes, we keep sending out agendas in advance, we circulate meeting minutes, and so on.

5. Quality communications. We make sure that everyone gets airtime at face-to-face or virtual meetings.

So, where's the problem?

The answer is that the listed items, done well, will ensure an effective team. But they won't produce an excellent team, a SuperTeam. The list focuses largely on the mechanics—that is, the management of teams.

SuperTeam Leadership

The difference between SuperTeam *leadership* and team *management* is critically important. Management is about creating structures and action plans; defining targets, expectations, and minimum standards; and then implementing them. It's about the mechanics including planning, monitoring, measuring, identifying shortfalls, and responding. It's about making things happen.

The leaders who work most effectively, it seems to me, never say "I." And that's not because they have trained themselves not to say "I." They don't think "I." They think "we"; they think "team." They understand their job to be to make the team function. They accept responsibility and don't sidestep it, but "we" gets the credit.... This is what creates trust, what enables you to get the task done.

—*Peter Drucker*

Leadership is about creating a long-term vision and a shared direction to reach it; ensuring that the team is well equipped to deliver it; inspiring the team to buy into the vision; enabling and engaging the team to develop appropriate strategies and plans; and defining and emulating the values and behaviors by which the team will live, in good times and in bad times.

Leadership's major impact is on values, on beliefs, on emotions, and on commitment. Many have documented the differences between leadership and management. In his 1989 book *On Becoming a Leader*, Warren Bennis composed one of the best lists of the differences between *management* and *leadership*. The following is a paraphrase of Bennis's and others' lists. Mark each item with an M or L to indicate whether you feel you are largely a manager or a leader:

_____ **1.** The manager gets things done. The leader visualizes and inspires.

_____ **2.** The manager replicates. The leader innovates.

_____ **3.** The manager sustains. The leader develops and enhances.

_____ **4.** The manager focuses on discipline and compliance. The leader focuses on people, energy, and commitment.

_____ **5.** The manager thinks about progress against the plan. The leader thinks what and why.

_____ **6.** The manager works in the business. The leader works on the business.

Forty-seven years after the event, Clinton can still remember one of his teachers at grammar school, Mr. John Caley. He led a group of 16-year-old boys, overnight, across miles and miles of rain-soaked Dartmoor in the United Kingdom as part of a Cadet training exercise—to be cheered at the end merely for advising that, because the group had succeeded, they would all get a cup of hot chocolate!

They were cold; they were tired; they had not eaten; they were wet. And he had made them do this apparently pointless task! Yet, they cheered him, merely for a cup of hot chocolate? No. They cheered him because he had led them to the end, believed in them despite their moaning and whining, kept up their morale by repeatedly describing the end point, enabled them to achieve something they would never have done alone, repeatedly provided personal advice and encouragement, frequently recognized progressive achievement, and then gave them the credit for having achieved the goal! He led them, not managed them.

Three cheers for Mr. Caley!

Recognition

Managers monitor and measure the progress, share the results, and thank the individuals and the teams for their contributions.

Ineffective team leaders take credit for the work of others, ignore individuals, make assumptions, treat all team members the same when their needs, aspirations, and performance are different, and convey the impression that they think that team members should be grateful for their roles and for having such a smart boss.

Effective leaders make recognition personal. They explain why individuals have been made part of the team, why they have been given a certain assignment, or why they had the success that they have. Leaders understand the motivation needs of each individual and address those—for example, they provide public recognition to those who welcome it and more personal attention to those who do not.

SuperTeam leadership is not only about recognizing individual team members and the team as a whole. It is also about not "unrecognizing" them. (In other words, SuperTeam leaders do not ignore great contributions and immense efforts, and they make sure that they do not leave out anyone who has made similar contributions.)

How well do you demonstrate SuperTeam leader *recognition* to other team members?

Empowerment

Managers delegate, and they take into account capability and commitment to minimize risk and ensure delivery.

Ineffective team leaders feel a need for control. They resort to management processes to make things happen. They overindulge in "touching base" or "one-to-ones," explaining how these give them opportunities to help. All too often, these processes consume time, demoralize the individuals and thus the team, and impose substandard decisions on the team. Ineffective team leaders can also go to the other extreme and allow individuals too much freedom in decision making compared to the individuals' capabilities.

A former manager of Clinton once described empowerment this way: "I am giving you the freedom to do what I want you to do." He went on to explain, "I make sure that, when I have given you the authority to make choices and decisions, I know and trust that you will make them from a range that I would approve of." It worked!

Empowerment requires a combination of education and delegation—educating yourself on each team member's capabilities; and educating individual team members on the authority and responsibilities that each one has, and then making clear how you want them to go about using the empowerment that you have given them.

Effective team leaders empower team members to make decisions and get things done with minimal management or supervision.

SuperTeam leaders give team members explicit autonomy and decision-making responsibility, and these leaders challenge and encourage them to take appropriate risks and think "outside the box" to create novel solutions. Of course, managerial progress checks and redirections are made—but not to the extent that they undermine performance.

How well do you demonstrate SuperTeam leader *empowerment* to other team members?

Supportive Feedback

Managers establish routine reporting, one-to-one and team reviews of achievements and progress, and periodic updating of plans. They make things happen. Managers provide feedback to get things back on track.

Ineffective team leaders provide feedback when it suits them, often as a reaction to some shortfall, and occasionally to some success that is brought to their attention. They may occasionally provide feedback proactively, but such feedback is often bland. For example, "I need to see better quality coming out of your area."

Effective leaders use all contact opportunities to optimize performance and development. They seize on each conversation and use it, for example, to communicate a priority, to give a specific piece of feedback, or to collect some performance evidence. They provide feedback to team members and the team as a whole as a routine way of keeping the team sharply focused on its goals and maximizing its achievements.

SuperTeam leaders provide prompt feedback (about both positive observations and negative ones) that is welcomed and made use of. Team members actually seek feedback from the SuperTeam leader, knowing that it will focus on a priority, include specifics about what was observed and why it matters, and provide ideas for how they can improve. Is this how things work on your team?

How well do you demonstrate SuperTeam leader *supportive feedback* to other team members?

Partnering

Managers make things happen, and, when the demand is high, they step in and help with the work, find alternative resources, or review with the team how the work can be rescheduled.

Ineffective team leaders do not fully exploit the synergy that can be achieved by combining thinking and effort. They merely sum the parts, a bit like a human pyramid or a chess team.

Effective leaders look for opportunities to work with team members to foresee challenges and then to partner with them to investigate and explore better ways of doing things. They focus on sustaining team member ownership of accountabilities while also contributing positively in times of challenge.

A SuperTeam works like an outstanding orchestra—one from which there is evocative beauty that emanates when the individual instrument sounds are combined. The SuperTeam leader acts as an ally and advocate. The SuperTeam leader works with the team members to set them up for success. SuperTeam leaders know when to lead, but they also know when to share in the team's working; when to be the advocate; and when to grab hold of the metaphorical rope and shout, "Heave."

How well do you demonstrate SuperTeam leader *partnering* with other team members?

Expectations

Managers follow clear and agreed-upon processes for actively engaging team members in specifying objectives and assigning tasks. The manager ensures that each team member is clear about what is expected of him (results, tasks, behaviors, and development).

Ineffective team leaders fail to make expectations (individual and collective) clear and complete, or they change the expectations too often, or they make them unrealistic.

Effective team leaders ensure that team member roles and responsibilities are defined clearly and the workload is distributed equitably. Team members know precisely the standards by which their performance is evaluated, and they are held accountable for meeting their performance expectations. The leader focuses on getting team members to expect much more of themselves, to set their own goals higher, and to commit to achieving them.

SuperTeam leaders bring the vision alive. They work with the team (individually and collectively) to make sure that everyone knows, understands, and can describe precisely the expectations of the team and of them as individual team members. In so doing, they encourage and inspire their team to continuously look for opportunities to set higher targets for the team and for themselves. Through direction and coaching, they ensure that this clarity and commitment to those expectations are achieved with each team member.

How well do you demonstrate SuperTeam leader *expectations* to other team members?

Consideration

The manager pays attention to individual team members' needs and ensures that all team members are treated with courtesy, dignity, and, most importantly, fairness.

Ineffective team leaders fail to recognize that team members are humans, not machines; they will "work from home" themselves when they have something being delivered or a child off from school, but they frown on a team member who asks to leave early because her dog has been taken seriously ill. They place unreasonable demands on individual team members such as, "Let's all stay on tonight and finish this," without checking privately with individuals to find out what is workable for them. They treat team members as though their only concern should be for the team goals and supporting them as the leader; they get "expected commitment" out of proportion.

Effective team leaders and team members demonstrate consideration, caring, and thoughtfulness toward one another. They are understanding and supportive when a team member experiences personal problems.

SuperTeam leaders understand that emotional issues have a significant impact on morale, engagement, and sustained productivity. They take the time necessary to find out about the personal demands and pressures on their team members and to demonstrate that they care. Although they do not always accede to requests, they are consistently considerate, not merely sympathetic. They encourage team members to be considerate of one another.

I'm bilingual, speaking English and body language. I prefer the latter because I can speak it silently and without listening and while my back is turned.

—*Jarod Kintz,* It Occurred to Me

How well do you demonstrate SuperTeam leader *consideration* to other team members?

Trust

Managers ensure that they have data on which to base decisions, that they know the strengths and limitations of each of their team members, and that they know how performance is progressing compared with the plan. This information enables them to know when and when not to delegate work and when they need to look into things further. They ensure that their decisions and actions are evidence based.

Ineffective team leaders micromanage (or abdicate). They believe in controls, and they check up on things unnecessarily or they abdicate and trust those not worthy of it.

Effective leaders make personal assessments of whom they can genuinely trust and for what. They understand that allowing people to do what they have already proven they can do is not really trusting them; they understand that trust can be demonstrated only when consciously and deliberately taking a calculated risk. They understand the tremendous motivating power that trusting someone in that way has—how it can drive step change improvements—and they also understand the potential risks that they take themselves when trusting someone else with a really important task.

SuperTeam leaders demonstrate trust and confidence in team members' skills and abilities. Team members feel that their leader and fellow team members have their backs and that the team leader will "do right" by them. All parties keep their promises and commitments, and they take responsibility when they fail to do so. Team members and the team leader speak to one another, not about one another, and they deal with conflict constructively.

How well do you demonstrate SuperTeam leader *trust* to other team members?

Leadership Versus Management

A SuperTeam needs the appropriate combination of management and leadership because it is the combination that determines the ultimate results. (See Figure 12.1.)

Management is efficiency in climbing the ladder of success; leadership determines whether the ladder is leaning against the right wall.

—*Stephen Covey*

Low Management/Low Leadership

Such teams lack energy and focus. They meet and discuss and attempt to plan, but commitment soon fades and action is ineffective. The lack of leadership means that any initial excitement rapidly evaporates. If the team survives, it has a tendency to become a rather bureaucratic, inwardly directed group focused largely on survival.

High Management/Low Leadership

The team meets, and they discuss and agree on plans of action. Strong management ensures that the necessary tasks are undertaken

	Low	MANAGEMENT	High
High	The team is excited initially. Some early results are positive. Commitment wanes quickly.	The team gets started quickly, and results get better. The workforce is highly engaged. Team capability strengthens.
Low	The team struggles to start projects. Little happens. Results are disappointing.	The team makes some initial progress. There is no momentum. Bureaucracy strangles progress.

Note: the left axis is labelled **LEADERSHIP** *(High at top, Low at bottom); the bottom axis is labelled* **MANAGEMENT** *(Low at left, High at right).*

FIGURE 12.1 Leadership Versus Management

and the correct procedures are followed. However, weak leadership means that individual commitment and energy are low and eroding. Eventually, it is management that sustains any activity, in place of any genuine passion. Slowly, bureaucracy takes over, and a mechanical operation evolves.

Low Management/High Leadership

Strong leadership creates initial energy that kick-starts performance. The team members meet, and they discuss and agree on plans of action. Weak management, however, means that the plans are not well executed, timelines or quality targets are missed, and individuals don't share in the work. Eventually, the lack of attention to managing the core work means that the dream slowly dies. Only powerful communications from, the personal charisma of, or simple faith in the leader mask that decline in the early stages. Eventually, the dream can turn into a nightmare!

High Management/High Leadership

Strong leadership creates the initial energy that kick-starts performance. The team members meet, and they discuss and agree on plans of action. Strong management ensures that the necessary tasks are undertaken and the correct procedures are followed. Motivated by short-term successes, the team sets itself more challenging goals, and with a solid foundation of effective management, the team starts to achieve them. A virtuous circle can soon be established. The strong leadership will, through *partnering, consideration*, and *recognition*, keep in tune with the work and the people, and it will ensure that burnout is avoided and high performance is sustained.

On Your Playing Field

Think of a team of which you are a member or leader.

1. Is the team, and any teams that report to it, well-structured and resourced to deliver? If not, how does it need to be improved, and why?
2. Are there effective and efficient management processes in place to accomplish the following (check those that apply):
   _____ Develop and maintain team action plans
   _____ Acquire and allocate appropriate resources
   _____ Clarify and agree on individual team member performance expectations
   _____ Train and/or influence the development of team members
   _____ Monitor and measure team member performance in real time
   _____ Identify shortfalls and improvement opportunities, and plan to correct, avoid, or exploit them as appropriate
   _____ Reward and recognize individual team members for their and/or the team's performance
   _____ Hold team members accountable for their performance, including contributions to strengthening the team
   What do you need to attend to, and how will you do so?
3. List the team members and the last time that you provided each one with effective *recognition*—that is, recognition that was appropriate and provided in the way the individuals like to receive it. Who or what have you missed?

4. What do you need to do to improve the clarity that individual team members have over what they are empowered to do and to decide?
5. How are you going to ensure that you give appropriate and timely supportive feedback to each member of the team?
6. What have you done to demonstrate the importance of true partnering (beyond mere collaboration) among your immediate team members? Do you do anything that may undermine their belief that you are "on their side" in this?
7. What have you done to ensure that individual team members are clear about their roles and how they fit with yours and those of the other team members?
8. Think about your team members. Do you really know them personally? Do you know what they like, what they dislike, what other demands they are currently experiencing, and what their aspirations are?
9. Do you have confidence in what you know about the knowledge, skills, and abilities of each team member? Of which team members is this not true?
10. Do team members trust you to "do right" by them? How do you know?

Wrap-Up

SuperTeam leaders demonstrate an appropriate combination of leadership (developing and defining the team's long-term vision, mission, strategy, and values; inspiring people to buy in to achieving the team's goals; and equipping and enabling it to happen) and management (getting the job done).

They balance the two to suit the needs of the team as a whole, the work that needs to be accomplished, and the needs of the individual team members.

SuperTeam leaders lead with RESPECT, finessing their behaviors to optimize the effectiveness of their interactions with team members and with their own team leaders.

Up Next

No team can be successful if it operates with an "everyone for himself or herself" approach. Too little empowerment and a team is stifled. Too much, and it becomes anarchistic and dysfunctional.

In the next chapter, we explore the issue of respecting team rules.

CHAPTER 13 Respecting
the Rules

The young man knows the rules, but the old man
knows the exceptions.

—*Oliver Wendell Holmes*

Overview

Rules are not meant to be broken. They are also not meant to be
followed so rigidly as to interfere with common sense and progress.
Actually, more important than the specific rules are the principles
underlying them. In the words of Franklin D. Roosevelt: "Rules are
not necessarily sacred, principles are."

The RESPECT Model is about ingraining the principle that all
people should be treated with respect and dignity. The principles of
an organization are more commonly known as its "core values." (We
will use the two terms interchangeably.) Principles lead to rules. For
example, "Team members shall not endure any form of discrimination
or harassment." Sacred principles and core values form the foundation of a team's culture and should be vigilantly protected by its rules.

In this chapter, you will learn:

- The importance of articulating and committing to a set of
  guiding principles
- The importance of creating and applying the rules that
  support these principles and keep them alive

- A process to facilitate your team's own list of sacred principles and core values
- Why rules can actually reflect dysfunction
- Rules to make meetings dramatically more effective

As a starting point, take a moment to reflect on the following questions.

SUPERSTARTER QUESTIONS

1. What are the sacred principles of your team and organization?
2. What are the rules that govern your team and organization?
3. Does everyone adhere to and support these rules? Are people held accountable if they break them?
4. Are there policies and procedures that no longer make sense? If so, what are they? What can you do to get them reviewed and changed or eliminated?
5. Do team members know which rules and boundaries can be challenged, and are they encouraged to do so?

The Rules

Whether it is a team of children playing kickball or the U.S. military, teams need rules. Team rules set forth clear expectations of behavior and foster consistency and fairness. Rules make life predictable and lead to stability, which leads to a sense of safety. All organizations—whether government, business, religious, social, or nonprofit—depend upon their members following the rules. Revolutions occur when citizens no longer respect the rules of their government. Respect is a matter of survival for teams and organizations as much as it is for individuals.

If you've never read the *Rule of Saint Benedict*, you should. Written 1,500 years ago, the book provides specific rules by which to govern monastic communities. Its principles and tenets are as relevant today as they were in the sixth century. In fact, the book is a "how to" manual for managing and leading organizations.

Any organization that has survived for 1,500 years has something to teach us, and in this case, it is that getting the rules right matters. For example, and most relevant to building a SuperTeam, Benedict calls for the brethren to not only be obedient to the abbot and his officials but also to one another. Benedict believed in TeamWe players who respected one another.

Creating the Rules

Rules are the policies, procedures, processes, and practices by which an organization is governed. Ideally, the rules—or at least the basic ones—are thoughtfully created when the organization is established, along with a clear mission, a vision, and set of core values. Unfortunately, they rarely are. The reason, obviously, is that most organizations are started by entrepreneurs who, even if they thought of creating such rules, would decide they were unnecessary.

In 2003, Paul founded ColorMe Company, which manufactured children's arts and crafts products such as colorable greeting cards, T-shirts, and pillowcases. It was founded as a for-profit company with nonprofit intentions, and it was cited by the *Wall Street Journal* as exemplary in its generosity in donating to nonprofits. During the 15 years prior to starting ColorMe Company, Paul had worked in the field of organizational development as a trainer, consultant, and educator.

Starting his own company gave him the opportunity to put into practice what he had studied and preached. Thus, while he worked by himself during the first six months, he created, reworked, and tweaked the company's vision, mission, guiding philosophical principles, and team rules (see Appendix B). He obsessed over these documents because he knew they would be the most important he ever created—they would in fact, guide all company decisions.

Does your company have these critical documents in place? Are your values and rules clearly articulated? More importantly, do they actually drive the behavior and culture of your team?

Your Team's Sacred Principles and Rules

Needless to say, we cannot suggest the specific sacred principles your team should adopt. However, we can offer some guidelines that will help you in both creating and revising your team's rules. In fact, you may already have your team rules—they simply aren't clearly articulated. If this is the case, we do encourage you to get them written down.

We also believe in learning from others and not reinventing the wheel. Thus, spend some time looking at the founding documents of other organizations. (In Appendix B you will find these documents for ColorMe Company.) Remember, it is the principles of your organization that give rise to the rules.

SuperTips for Creating Your Team's Sacred Principles

1. Gather your team, and share with them the idea of sacred principles and their importance. Refer to any core values that may already be promoted by the organization.
2. Share examples of core values and sacred principles from other organizations.
3. Ask team members to identify any explicitly stated or intrinsically lived principles. Discuss the impact and importance of these on your team's culture and your team's ability to achieve their goals and objectives.
4. Ask your team whether there are any core values or principles that are stated by the organization but that are not being lived on your team. (Sadly, treating others with respect is often one of them.) What is getting in the way of their being adhered to? What impact does this nonadherence have on team functioning?
5. Have the team discuss and write down on a whiteboard the additional or modified core values and sacred principles to which they aspire.

6. Ask for volunteers to form a committee to further refine these values. (We suggest that the team leader not be part of this committee.)
7. Request the committee to present their revised values to the team within the next three weeks, at which point other team members may offer their thoughts.
8. The committee should meet within the next two weeks and make any final revisions.
9. Adherence to these core values and sacred principles should become a strict expectation. Team members must take responsibility for holding themselves and one another accountable.
10. If possible, these core values should become part of the performance review—if not for every team member, then certainly for the team leader.

After these principles are clearly identified, the team may pursue developing team rules and policies. These are the rules most commonly found in a company handbook. Here's the thing to remember about rules: if the core values and sacred principles are actually lived as part of the culture, rules really aren't necessary. If lots of new rules are being created or if the existing ones are being revised often, it is a sign of team dysfunction. Why? Because most rules are created or revised when something goes wrong—and the source of such revisions is often one individual or a small group of team members. In fact, rules most often punish those who play by them.

A great example is the collection of rules companies have been writing lately to cover the use of social media—these rules are being created because of those who abuse their use. Other examples of numerous rules being created or revised all at once include dramatic revisions in security measures due to the actions of a handful of terrorists.

Integrity has no need of rules.

—Albert Camus

Your Team's Meeting Rules

Have you ever left a meeting where team members said, "Wow, that was actually a worthwhile meeting"? In many organizations there are too many meetings, they last too long, they are extremely inefficient, and they are not particularly productive. (We imagine that many of you are nodding your heads in agreement.) Meetings often present an enormous opportunity to improve team functioning and efficiency. If you and your team members are looking to "find time," meetings are a good place to look.

On the short list of organizational best practices, the *morning huddle meeting* is near the top. If you're not familiar with the morning huddle, the idea is quite simple. The team leader and team members gather in a 10-minute stand-up meeting during which individual team members share any highlights from the prior day, what they are working on today, and, if necessary, what help they may need. The team leader shares any bigger-picture issues or news. (Team leaders should never underestimate the extent to which team members desire transparency and information.) If your team is not holding a morning huddle meeting—start tomorrow.

In an effort to help your team make the best use of your meeting time, we have created a set of SuperTeam Meeting Rules that we strongly encourage you to consider adopting:

Rule 1. Participants will arrive on time for meetings; if they are going to be late, they are to be in communication with the meeting facilitator as soon as possible. Likewise, participants who may need to leave early should communicate this to the facilitator in advance, and the facilitator will announce it at the beginning of the meeting.

Rule 2. Meetings will begin and end on time.

Rule 3. The use of smartphone devices is prohibited unless possible urgent situations may arise and are communicated in advance.

Rule 4. Every meeting must have an established purpose with stated goals. Meetings should not be held strictly to provide information that could easily be communicated by other means—for example, via e-mail.

Rule 5. Meeting agendas and relevant information are to be distributed and read in advance to facilitate efficiency, unless such information could be misinterpreted or it is potentially volatile.

Rule 6. Meetings will begin with a review of the agenda and, if relevant, notes and commitments from the prior meeting.

Rule 7. Meetings will have a scribe responsible for note-taking and the distribution of those notes within 48 hours.

Rule 8. Meetings will have an identified timekeeper responsible for keeping to the schedule. Individuals will take responsibility for sticking to their time limits. Going over one's time should be viewed as highly unprofessional. Should a team member anticipate the need for greater time on the agenda, he or she should request this time in advance.

Rule 9. Meetings will have a gatekeeper who is responsible for ensuring that meetings stay focused and on track and who is responsible for posting off-track topics on a separate flipchart. The gatekeeper will also be responsible for managing participants who ramble.

Rule 10. Participants will direct their attention to the person speaking, and the speaker will establish eye contact with those listening. It is strongly recommended that paper handouts be limited as they encourage participants to look down and read.

Rule 11. "Yes, but . . ." will not be uttered.

Rule 12. No team member will say that an idea will not work without offering an alternative.

Rule 13. Meeting topics should be pertinent to everyone present. If some topics are not pertinent to everyone, a separate meeting should be arranged or those topics should be scheduled in such a way that individuals are allowed to leave once the content of the meeting is no longer relevant to them.

Rule 14. Meetings will conclude with a high-level review of the meeting, a review of any decisions that have been made, and a review of any agreed-upon assignments to individuals and the time frames for those assignments.

On Your Playing Field

Do you attend too many meetings that don't justify the time they take? If you're the person calling or facilitating the meeting, we urge you to adopt the rules we've listed in this chapter. If you're a participant in such meetings, we encourage you to share the rules with the facilitator and present him or her with the rationale that the rules will make the meetings more efficient and productive. Don't just sit there and grin and bear poorly led meetings!

Wrap-Up

We hope that, as a result of having read this chapter, you have a good sense of the critical importance of formulating and articulating your team's core values and sacred principles and that you see how they create the foundation of a SuperTeam culture. Teams function best when everyone knows the rules and is committed to them. We also hope that you will take away some tips that you can use to make your team meetings more effective.

Up Next

Now that we have discussed the foundation on which a team should be built, we will continue in the next chapter building the team!

CHAPTER 14 # Building a SuperTeam

> I think the players win the championship, and the
> organization has something to do with it, don't get
> me wrong. But don't try to put the organization
> above the players.
>
> —*Michael Jordan*

Overview

Determine the goals, select a leader, pick a team of people with the needed skills, equip them with the resources and tools they need, put processes in place to plan and manage the work, and communicate well . . . That's it!

What could go wrong with that?

In any type of team, the answer is, "Lots and lots and lots of things can go wrong . . . and usually do!"

In this chapter, we explore specifically what differentiates SuperTeam players and how to select them.

SUPERSTARTER QUESTIONS

Think of teams to which you belong now or to which you have belonged in the past:

156

1. Why did you join?
2. Based on what criteria were the team members identified and selected?
3. Were there team members who should not have been on the team? Why should they not have been selected?
4. Based on your experience, what would you look for in an ideal team member or team leader for a SuperTeam?
5. If your current team did not exist and you had to create it, how would you do it so that it would quickly become a SuperTeam?
   - How would you assess candidates to see if they are right for the team?
   - Whom would you involve in the selection process, and why?
   - How would you find out if your preferred candidates really want to be on the team?

TEAM ASSESSMENT

Instructions: Read each statement below, and, using the following scale, decide how accurately it describes your team:

Strongly disagree: 0 points
Disagree: 1 point
Agree: 2 points
Strongly agree: 3 points

Place the point value of your answer choice on the blank line at the beginning of each of the following statements:

_____ 1. **When we recruit new team members or leaders, we define precisely the skills we need them to have to do the job and to make, or keep, us a SuperTeam.**

_____ 2. **When we recruit new team members, we consider very seriously the people we already have on the team and how the new team members will need to fit in.**

_____ 3.   We assess the potential new team members' skills in working with others on a team, not merely their technical skills.

_____ 4.   We use only skilled assessors and proven tools for selection; we don't treat selection lightly.

_____ 5.   We conduct reviews of new recruits to learn what went well and what went less well during the selection process.

_____   Total score

INTERPRETING YOUR SCORES

0 to 5:   Your team needs to review its recruitment processes because you are not getting the best possible new team members you can. You may be missing job skills or at least the skills to make your team a SuperTeam.

6 to 10:   Your team has some of the basics right, but there is plenty of room for improvement. You probably have a mix of those who fit in and those who can do the job really well but not many who can do both.

11 to 15:   Your team appears to understand how to build a SuperTeam. Go back and look at the questions where you did not score 3. Keep reading because, in this chapter, we give you ideas on how to close that final gap.

ASSESSMENT REFLECTION EXERCISE

Whenever someone leaves the team, the pressure is always on "to put a butt on the seat." Yet, doing that alone can make things worse.

SuperTeam players are not merely good at doing their job. Many great individual players have failed to help their teams win; we see this on sports teams all the time. SuperTeam players add to the team cohesion, to the collective desire to win, to the willingness to go the extra mile to achieve success, and to the spirit of camaraderie.

Being underresourced is an issue, but being resourced with resources that don't work well together can reduce overall capacity and make everybody's life more difficult. Don't take second best for expediency because it will almost always end in grief . . . for you and for them!

Think about the last person added to your team:

1. What worked well? Which steps of the process brought this person to the fore?
2. What about this person really added value to the team?
3. Who was instrumental in the selection process—that is, in finding and singling out this person?

Selecting the Members of a SuperTeam

It is difficult to build even a mediocre team! Building a SuperTeam requires a super effort.

There are five rules for selecting members of a SuperTeam:

Rule 1. Make sure that you need a team. Yes, make sure that what needs to be done really will be best accomplished by a team. If not, then create the best role to get the work done and move on. Teams are not the answer to everything.

Rule 2. Get the right leader—someone who is fully committed to the team's goals and to leading and managing a SuperTeam. Search for a team leader who clearly believes in the team's goals; who is articulate; who can bring the future alive; who knows what great teamwork looks like and the types of people who work excellently together; who can engage skilled team members and bring out the best in them; and who will monitor progress and take corrective action when needed. Select a team leader who is passionate about growing and developing others and not afraid to work themselves out of a job.

Rule 3. Get the right technical skill sets on the team—that is, the capabilities necessary to complete the tasks needed to achieve the goals.

Great leadership, effort, and team-working skills cannot compensate for the lack of technical competence or technical resources. Someone has to do the work properly! Getting the right people is often more important than getting the number of people right.

Regarding capability, sufficient technical competence in the team maximizes the independence of the team and the probability of its success. Be prepared to pay a fair rate to get what you need.

Rule 4. Get excellent team-working skills. Teams typically fail merely because the team members are unable to work together effectively. You need people with that X Factor! For SuperTeam members, you are looking for the natural desire to live by the RESPECT Model. You need team members who have a proven track record in working with other people:

- **Recognizing** the contributions of others as a way of building collaborative working relationships and encouraging others to perform at their best—someone more focused on giving credit than taking it.
- **Empowering** others to make significant contributions— not controlling assignments and keeping the good bits for themselves.
- Providing **supportive feedback** to others to enable them to succeed—not viewing their role as to pick up the pieces or criticize.
- **Partnering** with people when they need support and guidance; when the work needs that combined effort; and when there is a chance to "cross the finish line together"— not abdicating or becoming dictatorial when the going gets tough.
- Setting **expectations** clearly for others so that misunderstandings about what needs to be done are minimized and others can get on with their work—not leaving things ambiguous or frequently moving the goalposts unexpectedly.
- Showing **consideration** when others have personal issues or challenges that impact what would be the normal way of working together, and demonstrating empathy when appropriate to sustain a cohesive team—not applying bland rules to everyone or, worse still, having one rule for oneself and another rule for everyone else.
- **Trusting** others until genuinely proved wrong, and also of being trusted. Beware of those who explain the

prior failure of bosses or organizations to give them responsibility. There might have been a reason. Just check!

As many have put it, "Hire for attitude and train for skill." What you know and can do can change, but who you are is fixed! **Rule 5. Take out the bad apples.** Building a SuperTeam is largely about finding and keeping the right people. However, all selection processes are flawed, and "one bad apple can make a whole barrel rotten." One of the most common and detrimental mistakes that team leaders make is keeping poor performers. Do not procrastinate over exiting an unacceptable team member.

The SuperTeam Ingredients

Groups of people do not always become teams; many remain groups of people who don't really come together as a team, and some groups disintegrate completely. Because RESPECT is the major driver of sustained engagement and productivity in SuperTeams, the challenge is to attract and select candidates who will "close the circle of respect" (as Paul so aptly articulates in his prior book, *Carrots and Sticks Don't Work*):

- They respect the team itself. They see why there is a team, and they understand its inherent value and how it is set up to operate. They believe in the team that you are considering them to join. They don't just want to play—they want to play on THIS team.
- They respect the team leader. They see the value that he or she adds, and, if in doubt, they trust and support the leader's judgment and decisions. If they don't know the team leader, then you need to know the *type* of team leader they respect.
- They respect their fellow team members. They respect each other for who they are, not merely for what they do and how they do it. If they don't know the other team members, then you need to know the *type* of team members they respect.
- They respect the work they will be asked to do. Every job has its great components and its dross! You need team members who will respect everything that they are required to do, or

they will, within the workings of the team, partner with you to improve it.

- They feel respected. This has two components. One, they ARE respected. You need team members whom others will respect. Second, they need to feel respected—some people are just not good at that. They are either overly self-deprecating or just plain insecure. Neither helps with building a SuperTeam. You don't want arrogance, but you do want pride based on confidence. Great team players look for the positive in their team experiences, and this reinforces their feeling of being respected. They take steps to ensure that other team members feel the same way.

This circle of RESPECT only arises and continues when the right people come together and interact in the appropriate ways.

So, what should you look for? Here are some practical ideas.

Respect for the Team

A major source of frustration in any group of people is when others join voluntarily, presumably because they want to, and then they immediately start to criticize the team. Of course, they always argue that they want to improve things, but we can all tell when their motives are entirely selfish.

This attitude is not something that can be changed easily after recruitment. Those with it soon become naysayers and a burden.

"So, John. Thanks for coming in today. I'm delighted to get the chance to speak with you myself. Tell me why you'd like to join the internal audit team?"

"Sure. It's not so much the audit team that I want to join. From the last divisional report, it looks like the team needs to up its game, and I think I can make that happen. Assuming I do, I believe that this could be a good move for me, hopefully into a divisional management accounting role."

Hmm. He's going to be a great guy to have around—I don't think so!

When recruiting new team members, find out if they genuinely believe in the team and their potential role in it. Or are they merely looking for a job, any job? One who sees the role as primarily a stepping-stone to another role can prove to be a disaster, especially if you make that person the team leader. When talking about a former team, do they focus merely on what they did and got out of it, or do they recognize the value of the team and the other team members?

If you are trying to recruit into an existing team, your reputation will go before you. If you have an excellent team, people will want to join. Make sure that people outside of the team, especially potential recruits, get to hear about the benefits of being part of your team. This is an important public relations challenge.

QUESTIONS ABOUT RESPECT FOR THE TEAM If you are contemplating creating or adding to a SuperTeam, here are some questions you might ask candidates. Then listen for evidence of some of the above issues in their responses:

> Tell me what you know about the team and why it exists.
> Could we achieve the same results without a team? Would you
>   recommend that?
> Why is this specific team important?
> What do you see as the purpose of the team?
> What value do you see in what the team delivers?
> Give me an example of when your team was asked to do
>   something with which you disagreed. How did you
>   handle that?

Respect for the Team Leader

Leaders can be effective only if they have enthusiastic followers. Leading is about getting people doing what is needed of them because they want to do it.

In SuperTeams, team members believe in the role of the leader, and they trust the current leader.

Respect is not about blind obedience. In SuperTeams, respect for the leader is demonstrated by doing what is expected, albeit sometimes after fact-based and frank dialogue. Respect for the leader can be demonstrated by challenging the leader openly and honestly and not ignoring, spreading rumors about, undermining, or aggressively confronting him or her.

When recruiting new team members, it is often difficult to evaluate the respect that they have for the current or intended team leader. However, it is relatively easy to check out candidates' respect for the role of team leader and their respect for any prior team leaders with whom they have worked.

"Yan, as you know, we are also in the process of hiring a new team leader. Tell me a little about your expectations of that person, assuming you get the job you are applying for on the team."

Which of the following answers do you feel suggests a stronger respect for the role of team leader?

1. Frankly, I really don't mind. I believe that I can do what is required of me, and I won't need much supervision. As long as the leader can ensure that I have the information and tools that I need, I can work with anyone.
2. Hmm. Good question. Based on my experience, we need someone who, when things go wrong, can get the situation sorted out for us so that we can get on with our jobs.
3. I hope the team leader is going to get us all on the same page, work though any differences of opinion, and get everyone excited about and committed to achieving amazing results.

The latter response indicates someone who understands that the role of the leader is to lead, not abdicate, and also to bring the team together to commit to common goals.

QUESTIONS ABOUT RESPECT FOR THE TEAM LEADER If you are contemplating creating or adding to a SuperTeam, here are some questions you might ask candidates. Then listen for evidence of some of the above issues in their responses:

Tell me about your last or current team leader.

What do you look for in a team leader?

Describe a team leader you really admired.

Describe a team leader you did not admire.

What should a team member do if her team leader falls short?

How important is the role of team leader, and why?

Give me an example of when your supervisor or team leader has treated you with disrespect. What did he do? What did you do?

Respect for the Other Team Members

There is no "I" in "team," but there is in "win."

—*Michael Jordan*

In the same way that it takes time to develop respect for the leader, the same is true for fellow team members. Such respect can also be shattered in the casting of a scowl in a team meeting or in the spreading of a rumor in the restroom!

In SuperTeams, individual team members understand the critical importance of **mutual respect**; they know that a team is only as strong as its weakest link.

If one of the team members does something that is viewed as unusual or unacceptable, fellow team members raise the issue, and they provide clear, honest, and behaviorally focused feedback. They offer help and advice to move forward. In SuperTeams, individual team members know when to ask for help, and they don't feel uncomfortable about doing so. They know they will receive help unconditionally.

In SuperTeams, members make sacrifices for the good of the team. In SuperTeams, members respect one another because they believe that mutual respect is the mark of a civilized society, not merely because they are paid to work together.

When recruiting new team members, explore their views of others. Do they naturally look for the strengths in others, or do they always see the deficiencies? Do they view the provision of service to others as something to be valued or as a sign of subservience? Do they look for ways to define themselves as superior to others, or do they view all as having value? Do they ask about the strengths of their potential peers?

QUESTIONS ABOUT RESPECT FOR OTHER TEAM MEMBERS If you are contemplating creating or adding to a SuperTeam, here are some questions you might ask candidates. Then listen for evidence of some of the above issues in their responses:

Tell me about your current fellow team members.
What do you look for in your fellow team members?
What do you bring to any team to which you belong?
How would others describe you as a team member?
Give me an example of someone on a team with whom you found it very difficult to work. How did you handle that?

Respect for the Work

Being part of a team and then not executing the plays does not produce stellar performance. Obsessive commitment to getting the job done may sound like a harsh demand, but it is this demonstration of respect for the work that characterizes truly exceptional team players.

So, ask the candidates to talk about the job and what it means to them. Listen for evidence that they genuinely believe in what they will be asked to do and what the team as a whole does. Check their understanding of what it takes not merely to succeed but to excel. Listen for evidence that they believe that excelling, not merely succeeding, really matters. Listen for evidence that they share the values that the team needs to live by. Listen especially for evidence that they understand that they will need to excel individually, not merely be part of a team that does.

Sue was nervous. She so wanted this job. It was really close to home. It was a great company that prided itself on the quality of the food it produced and the fact that it sourced produce locally. The pay was good, and the company seemed to be growing, so the job should be secure. She had done her homework, and she knew that she could answer most questions likely to come up about the type of work she'd be doing on the finance team:

"So, Sue. Thanks for that. It seems that you have a good grasp of the work that you'd likely be doing. We are interviewing a number of candidates, and I expect that most will also have the technical skills we need. Tell me, why do *you* want this job?"

"I'm looking for a job that can help me improve my accounting skills. I am especially interested in learning about corporate finance and how companies acquire funding. I'd love to be able to do that. Also, this job's really local so I'll get to spend more time with my family rather than traveling. And it seems like a great company to work for—all the people I have met have been really friendly. There seems to be a real sense of teamwork."

So she's keen to learn, and she seems energetic and enthusiastic. She's local so she won't have travel and time issues. She seems to like people, and she wants to get along with them. What's the problem?

Yes, she's keen. However, she is keen about what she can do and achieve, and she is keen to get home. She's keen to work with nice people—aren't we all! Where is the commitment to what she will have to do and what the team does—no mention of it at all? Where is the evidence that making a contribution to others is something she values? She appears to be somewhat of a TeamMe player.

QUESTIONS ABOUT RESPECT FOR THE WORK If you are contemplating creating or adding to a SuperTeam, here are some questions you might ask candidates. Then listen for evidence of some of the above issues in their responses:

Describe what you believe you will be required to do.
What do you hope you will not have to do?
What value does the work of the team add?

What type of work do you not like doing?

What type of work do you like doing?

Describe a situation in which you have had to do something that you considered unnecessary or not appropriate. What did you do?

Feeling Respected

As we said above, this has two components: they ARE respected, and they FEEL respected. Many of us remember being dumped on and then told afterward that what we did was appreciated . . . and so we were left feeling that we had been both patronized and used!

How can you predict that someone has a sufficiently positive attitude to both earn respect and feel it when they get it? Some people always see the glass as half full, and so they are more likely to feel respected. Some people always see the glass as half empty, and so they more often feel disrespected.

Ask candidates about their recent team experiences. Listen for evidence that they were given significant responsibility and given reasonable autonomy. Listen to hear whether others sought their help, support, and/or counsel. Those do not happen if you are not respected.

Listen for evidence of how they take positive messages out of their experiences—for example, did they see responsibility as a positive or as "more work." Or listen for how they twist things to make out that they were taken advantage of—for example, "The only reason they gave that to me was that they knew I would clean up the mess."

QUESTIONS ABOUT FEELING RESPECTED If you are contemplating creating or adding to a SuperTeam, here are some questions you might ask candidates. Then listen for evidence of some of the above issues in their responses:

How important to you is it that other team members respect you?

What have others liked about what you have done on their teams?

How do you judge your contributions to a team?

What do you expect from other team members?

What shows you that others respect you?

Give me an example of when you have not liked or you have been at odds with a fellow team member. What did you do or say?

What impact does it have if others do not respect you?

Engaging the Team in Team Member Selection

Involving other members of the team, or even other stakeholders, in the selection of new team members can achieve a number of positive results:

- A better decision and thus better additions to the team. Some organizations are even using the concept of crowdsourcing in recruitment.
- A higher level of commitment from the existing team to receiving the new team members.
- The candidates can make a more considered decision about whether or not to join the team.

Consider setting up an opportunity for the potential new team members to join the team and work on something very practical or to engage with them in a debate about a real task; treat either as work experience.

Will what you observe be truly predictive of how they will perform if added to the team? NO. But it will be way better than most other indicators. It will also be a good opportunity for unsuitable candidates to select themselves out of the process.

Will all of your current team members be good at selection? NO. But you can train them, and, again, multiple opinions may at least trigger debate about the evidence.

Too Many on the Benches

Being underresourced has become a badge of honor for recession-era managers; they boast to their colleagues about how they have cut costs by not replacing people on their team. Of course, the payback comes when peaks occur: the remaining team members burn out, service and delivery suffer, morale declines, and attrition rises.

However, the opposite can also be bad. Managers who fill their teams with resources that are superfluous to the requirements of the work at hand also experience problems. Team members are not challenged, growth opportunities are few, and discontent flourishes (they have time to spread it!).

There are not more than five musical notes; yet the combinations of these five give rise to more melodies than can ever be heard. There are not more than five primary colors; yet in combination they produce more hues than can ever be seen. There are not more than five cardinal tastes; yet combinations of them yield more flavors than can ever be tasted.

—*Sun Tzu,* The Art of War

Cleaning Up the House

In the world of teamwork, there are few sins worse than keeping underperforming team members. Of course, leaders must clarify expectations, provide feedback, create opportunities to improve, and share evaluations. But do not procrastinate over exiting a poor performer. Your team is only as strong as its weakest, not its strongest, link.

Collect evidence, decide, act, and move on.

On Your Playing Field

Think about your team (current or new), and prepare to take on people who will make it excel and become a SuperTeam:

1. Do you have clear job descriptions for the roles? If not, complete them.
2. Do you understand the knowledge, skills, and competencies needed to excel in each role? If not, complete these job holder criteria.

3. Do you know how and do you have the capability or resources to shortlist those candidates who can do the specific tasks needed by the team? If not, work out how to do so.
4. Do you have the capability to shortlist those candidates who have the ability to work as part of a team? If not, work out how to do so.
5. Do you have the capability to make the final selection based on the candidates' ability to live the RESPECT Model? If not, work out how to do so.

Wrap-Up

1. Make sure that your team is successful and that it has a positive public image. This will encourage talented people to want to join the team.
2. Great individual skills do not compensate for a lack of team-working skills or appropriate attitudes.
3. Check out the candidates' beliefs in the value of the team; their respect for team leadership; their respect for their peers; and their respect for the work they have to do or will have to do. Also check out whether they have a positive attitude that is likely to support their feeling valued in the team.
4. Actively engage team members and possibly stakeholders in recruitment decisions.
5. As early as possible, exit those team members who do not fit.

Up Next

Organizations and teams frequently select excellent candidates and then seriously mishandle bringing the new team members on board.

Can you remember one of those occasions when you were paraded through the building like a prize-winning steer? When you had dozens of names thrown at you? When you were not given the opportunity to converse beyond the most trivial of small talk? If so, read on—the next chapter about onboarding is for you!

CHAPTER 15

Bringing New Members into the Team

> The Romans thought of themselves as the chosen people, yet they built the greatest army on Earth by recruiting warriors from any background.
>
> —*Amy Chua*

Overview

Teams rarely remain the same; team members and leaders come and go. In this chapter, we explore those team dynamics—the challenges associated with bringing new members into a team and catering to new cultural dimensions, interests, and expectations.

SUPERSTARTER QUESTIONS

1. What are the concerns that new team members have?
2. Think of an occasion when you joined a team and it was a very positive experience. Why was that? What happened that made you feel so good?
3. Think of an occasion when you joined a team and it was an unpleasant or unrewarding experience. Why was that? What happened that made you feel poorly?

4. What can you do to make new team members' entry a really positive experience that sets them up for success?

TEAM ASSESSMENT

Instructions: Read each statement below, and, using the following scale, decide how accurately it describes your team:

Strongly disagree: 0 points
Disagree: 1 point
Agree: 2 points
Strongly agree: 3 points

Place the point value of your answer choice on the blank line at the beginning of each of the following statements:

_____ 1. **When we receive new team members, the team leader and the team members make sure that the new team members' first experiences are positive.**

_____ 2. **The current team members take steps to ensure that new team members feel useful quickly. We equip them with the knowledge and tools they need to succeed, and we give them things to do that are clearly valuable.**

_____ 3. **The team takes time to understand the new team members and any new ideas they bring.**

_____ 4. **The team takes time to understand the new team members and what additional knowledge and skills they add.**

_____ 5. **The team engages with the new team members to understand what their needs are, what their expectations are, and what they need to be successful.**

_____ **Total score**

INTERPRETING YOUR SCORES

0 to 5: Your team is probably not bringing out the best in new team members. New team members may be getting into their job, but they are probably not getting into the team. There may well be cliques or pockets in the team, and whether new members get adopted easily depends on pure chance.

6 to 10: Your team has some of the basics right, but there is plenty of room for improvement. You are seeking to create a positive team working environment, but you may not be doing all you can to engage new members. It is still up to them "to work out when to run onto the field" and where they fit in the team.

11 to 15: Your team appears to understand team onboarding. New team members are set up for success, and they rapidly become one of the team. If you don't already have SuperTeam status in terms of connectedness, you are close.

ASSESSMENT REFLECTION EXERCISE

Most organizations have formal onboarding processes. These largely attend to the organization's needs—for example, the legal paperwork such as the signing of nondisclosure agreements (NDAs).

Most onboarding processes also attend to the critical needs of the individuals—for example, desk, employee ID, tour of the work area, provision of equipment, and log-in details.

Far fewer onboarding processes approach the issue from the new team members' personal perspective. This is where attention to the RESPECT Model can elevate the positive impact of any onboarding exercise. Think about the last few new team members:

1. Were you well prepared for them when they arrived? Or was it hurried and you had to find someone "to look after them"?
2. How well do you and each of the other team members know the new team members as people, not merely as team members? Are they genuinely already equal members of the team, or are they still the "newbies"?

3. How quickly is it before team members instinctively "cover the backs" of the new team members in their absence, not merely when they are around?

4. Would those outside of your team describe you as a great team, a collection of coworkers, or a clique?

Respectful Onboarding

When selecting new team members, we are not only asking if the candidates can do the specific jobs or if they can work well in this team. We are also asking whether the existing team will accept the new members. Whether they do so is not only determined by the candidates—it is also determined by the existing team and how they receive the new team members. In the last chapter, we recommended involving the team in the selection process as one step toward addressing this challenge.

Effective onboarding can increase the success rate of new team members or a new team leader, and it can also reduce significantly the ramp-up time needed for them to reach SuperTeam player status.

Hopefully, you will attend to all of the normal onboarding issues like legal paperwork, desk, equipment, introductions, and the locations of the restrooms. But consider adding the following steps to your repertoire because with them, you can turn the onboarding process into a launch pad for SuperPerformance.

If there are new members joining your team, demonstrate RESPECT early.

Recognition

Early recognition can help build confidence. The following steps are important if new team members are to actively engage with the team and the work:

1. Before they arrive, make sure that the existing team members know something about them—especially anything that may affect how they will work with the existing members—for example, any special needs, any strong preferences, any

personal circumstances that may impact work, or any passions such as cycling, kayaking, dancing, or music.

2. Specifically welcome them, and greet them by name (as they like to be greeted—for example, "Chris" rather than "Christine"). Say your own name slowly so they get it, and provide a thumbnail sketch: "This is me."

3. Make sure that everyone else on the team greets them that way too.

4. You should know enough about the new team members to be able to recognize sincerely and explicitly what they bring to the team. Focus on positives they can add. Explain how they will link with the existing strengths. But, don't talk yet about team shortfalls they will fix (unless this is specifically why they were hired). That may well make others feel disrespected.

5. Look for real opportunities to recognize their contributions early on. It is all too easy to ignore new team members in their early days and when the heat is on. However, don't flatter for the sake of it either—you will embarrass them and annoy the existing team members. Give the new team members recognition, give them a chance to add value, and avoid setting them up to fail:

> "Chris, this is something you may be able to comment on. I recall that in your last job, you led the team that successfully implemented real-time mirrored server back-ups. What would you advise we do or consider here?"

Empowerment

Clarifying the specific level of empowerment enables new team members to get up to speed quickly in terms of knowing what they can do on their own authority, without checking first with the team leader or other team members. This is very important. Adding new team members typically weakens the team initially as the existing team members have to do their own work, and train the new hires and answer their questions:

1. Give the new team members all the useful information they will need. For example, whom do they call when the toilet

overflows? What should they do if they set off the alarm when coming in early or leaving late? Where are the printer supplies kept? Whom should they go to with personal issues?

2. Make sure that the new team members know what they have the authority to do:
   - What can they do without checking in with other team members or the team leader—unless there's an issue?
   - Do they need to keep others up to date on what they have decided and/or what they have done? Whom should they inform?

3. Make sure that they know who can approve their actions if their normal supervisor is not available and something needs authorizing.

Supportive Feedback

Supportive feedback is an integral part of any effective continuous improvement process and should be clearly explained during the onboarding process:

1. Agree with new team members how you will be kept informed by them of their progress.
2. Agree with new team members how you will keep them informed of how you view their progress.
3. Agree with new team members how fellow team members will give feedback on their progress.
4. Ask the new team members what they'd most like to receive feedback on.
5. Advise them, based on what you learned during the selection process, on what you feel they could most benefit from in terms of feedback from you and from others. Suggest that they ask for that feedback from others when appropriate.
6. Provide the new members with early clear, specific, and constructive feedback especially on how they are working with the team. Help them to accelerate their integration.

Partnering

Partnering is about making the new hires more than members of the team. It is about integrating them into the team and making them key players:

1. Demonstrate partnering. Play an active role in introducing them to the team; don't delegate it.
2. Partner with them to plan how they are going to engage promptly in some team activity. Find early wins.
3. Have the existing team members partner with the new team members on specific aspects of their training and explain to them the importance the team places on partnering (which is much stronger than collaborating).
4. Introduce them to other departments and people with whom they will interact, and explain how they can partner with these people when appropriate.

No matter whether you are a new or an old team member, you need time to adjust to one another.

—Yao Ming

Expectations

Expectations are about clarity—avoiding misunderstandings, avoiding duplicated effort, avoiding "crossed wires," maximizing synergies, and keeping everyone aligned and on point. Make the new team members' roles clear.

1. Tell, explain, and check their understanding of **what they are expected to achieve** individually, as well as with the team.
2. Tell, explain, and check their understanding of **what they are expected to do** in the first few days on the team.
3. Tell, explain, and check their understanding of **how they are expected to engage with** and work in the team, including the values by which the team operates.
4. Tell, explain, and check their understanding of **what they are expected to do if they need help**: "If in doubt, ask for it."
5. Tell, explain, and check their understanding **that they are expected to RESPECT everyone**.

6. Tell, explain, and check their understanding **that they are expected to help others**. Team success is greater than the sum of individual successes.

Consideration

Consideration is about caring for one another as well as for the work. It is about being sensitive to the fact that, no matter what happens or who we are, there are things outside of the team that affect us—we are human beings, and those human feelings unavoidably impact how we think and act. SuperTeams get that and work with it:

1. Don't assume the new team members know anything. Show them around and where to find the things they may need. But be sensitive enough not to patronize—watch for those "I know!" looks.
2. Introduce them and give them some notes and even photos by which to remember what they are told. (Can you remember names after the third person you are introduced to in a short space of time?)
3. Share the written and, more important, the unwritten rules—who sits and parks where, who organizes lunch, or who is the best person to contact for certain issues.
4. Help the new team members avoid putting their foot in their mouth by your sharing any current sensitivities that are *not* confidential—for example, this team member has a sick relative, this team member has been in a recent car accident, and so on.
5. Give them a lexicon of colloquialisms, acronyms, or pet names.
6. If existing team members have business cards, give the new team members their own business cards on day 1 so they can give theirs out when presented with others' cards. (Do you remember how embarrassing it is to have to keep saying, "Oh, sorry. I don't have my business cards yet"?)

In an early career move, Clinton joined a small company. The company did not yet have proper offices, and it worked from the owner's friend's apartment.

Late on the night before his first day in the new role, Clinton took a call from his new boss: "Hi. Sorry, I won't be able to be there tomorrow, Clint. Drop by my house, and my wife will give you the office key. Get yourself settled. There are lots of proposals in the bookcase. Spend the day getting familiar, and I'll catch up tomorrow. Thanks. OK?"

"Sure."

The next night: "Clint. Hi. I am so embarrassed. You are not going to believe this, but I can't make it again tomorrow. Look. I know what. Can you go out and see if you can find some really good desks—I want ones with larger-than-usual tops so we can spread stuff out. See you tomorrow."

The next night, his wife rang: "Clint. Hi. I know this is not funny but . . ."

"Don't tell me. He can't make it tomorrow either. Look, I know things crop up, but I am getting rather concerned, and I think I may have made a bad decision. What's going on? Do you know?"

"Yes. Didn't he tell you? He entered into a tennis tournament with his friend—the one whose apartment you are using as the office. Well, it seems that the field is a bit weak. He keeps winning, and he is now into the semifinals tomorrow!"

To this day, Clinton can remember the emotions of each call of each morning and each evening. They have never gone away!

Trust

Trust is about creating an environment that is immensely effective and efficient where individuals don't need to keep checking up on things and they feel that their backs are covered when they are not there:

1. Don't expect the new team members to trust you or the team immediately. Remember that you have to earn trust and that you can lose it in a flash! Walk your talk! Always!
2. Find opportunities to trust the new team members. Actively focus on allowing them to show what they can do. The task is not to show how clever you are. It is to give them the chance to show how good they are!

Preparing for New Team Members

If you have a family, can you remember the lengths you went to before the baby arrived—thinking of names, buying supplies, preparing the nursery, equipping the kitchen, equipping the bathroom, and buying clothes for the first few months? Even if you don't have children, you have probably been bored mindless by the ravings of those who do! And, apart from the immeasurable pleasure babies bring, this baby is going to add little value to the team. Financially, it is going to be a "learning experience"!

So why is it that we wait until just a few days before they arrive to start thinking about new team members in our working environment? The instant of entry into your team world can be as startling as birth; it can have as long lasting implications as that first slap on the bottom or those first lung-clearing shrieks!

So, if you are contemplating creating a SuperTeam or adding new members to your team, consider the following:

1. What can I do to earn the respect of the new team members? What must I avoid doing that could inhibit that?
2. What can I do in advance or in the first few days to reinforce the perceived value of the team and how it works?
3. What can I do to maximize the probability that other team members will demonstrate genuine respect and to minimize the probability that they will undermine it?
4. What can I do to set up the new team members for quick wins and long-term successes?

On Your Playing Field

Look at your process for onboarding new team members, and identify where it can be improved. Make a plan to get that done.

Think about any recent new team members. What was missing in their onboarding? Can this be back-filled?

Wrap-Up

Effective onboarding of new team members is critically important, and it involves far more than merely enabling them to join the team.

Effective onboarding rapidly builds strong relationships within the team, and those relationships lubricate the team's work. Use your onboarding process to accomplish the following:

- Give the new team members the rules of play.
- Equip them for the unexpected.
- Set them up for success.
- Give them confidence. Recognize what they bring, and encourage them to contribute enthusiastically.
- Enable them to contribute quickly. Empower them to be a major contributor in a way that is suited to their abilities.
- Give them feedback so that they can polish any "rough edges" you noticed during recruitment. Support them early on with constructive feedback; reinforce good behavior, and address any shortfalls.
- Partner with them to get them firing on all cylinders. It is in your best interests to minimize their ramp-up time.
- Make your expectations of them and of the existing team members clear in relation to getting their feet under the table and operating as full team members.
- Show consideration for their personal needs without complicating other relationships within the team.
- Trust them until proven wrong, and earn their trust as quickly as you can.

Up Next

Well, you have the right team members, and you have them on board. You are ready to set sail! But is it all going to be clear sailing, or are there squalls on the horizon?

If you read Paul's last book, you will remember what he said: "Carrots and Sticks Don't Work." If you didn't read it, go buy a copy . . . NOW! No, seriously, you can wait until you have finished this book because, in the next chapter, we explore how to get that SuperTeam SuperPerforming.

CHAPTER 16

Excelling

> Of all the things I've done, the most vital is coordinating the talents of those who work for us and pointing them toward a certain goal.
>
> —*Walt Disney*

Overview

Assembling a team is difficult; there are many factors to be considered, some of which are much bigger than, "Can they perform the specific work?" Assembling a SuperTeam is even harder because we are seeking to get everyone working at maximum productivity with minimal supervision.

In the spring of 2013, the former England soccer team captain Rio Ferdinand and top player Wayne Rooney admitted that England's so-called golden generation simply hadn't been good enough to win a major tournament. Despite boasting some of the world's best players at five of the previous six major tournaments, the England team struggled to get even near the likes of Spain, Germany, Brazil, and Holland.

Some blamed the lack of a winter break in the Premier League and the tactical ineptitude of the managers for an immensely talented team not winning an international trophy. But Ferdinand tweeted: "Great players don't always make great teams."

In this chapter, we explore the challenge of maximizing individual performance and maximizing collective team performance.

SUPERSTARTER QUESTIONS

1. Think of a team that you considered to be performing less well than desired. Why was that? What was inhibiting their performance?
2. Think of a team that you considered to be performing extremely well—perhaps even better than believed possible. Why was that? What was driving their performance?
3. Think of a team whose performance you observed to change significantly one way or the other. Why was that? What happened to trigger and sustain the change?
4. Think of your own team. How good is its current performance (a) compared with expectation and (b) compared to what you believe is possible?

TEAM ASSESSMENT

Instructions: Read each statement below, and, using the following scale, decide how accurately it describes your team. As this chapter is largely about performance management, we are going to use a different scale (that was a joke—in most organizations, the way they often try to raise performance is by changing the rating scale!):

Strongly disagree: 0 points
Disagree: 1 point
Agree: 2 points
Strongly agree: 3 points

Place the point value of your answer choice on the blank line at the beginning of each of the following statements:

_____ 1. **Setting direction.** Our team has a clear and specific understanding of higher-level goals, plans, and organizational values. We know the priorities and how we are expected to operate to contribute to meeting them.

_____ 2. **Clarifying roles.** On our team, we ensure that individual team members have a clear understanding of their role in terms of the specific job as well as the role they are expected to play in the performance of the team as a whole.

_____ 3. **Planning and aligning performance.** In our team, we have and maintain detailed and comprehensive individual performance plans, and we ensure that these are tightly aligned to maximize our collective performance. The plans cover results, tasks, behaviors, and development needed.

_____ 4. **Monitoring and measuring performance.** In our team, we track progress, and we produce meaningful data on which to base change. The data brings objectivity to an otherwise subjective process, which lays the foundation for evaluation and appraisal. We monitor results, tasks, behaviors, and development.

_____ 5. **Enabling and enhancing performance.** In our team, we focus on improving performance. We address the critical performance factors of capability—for example, training or coaching; opportunity—for example, access, resources, or empowerment; and inclination—for example, job satisfaction, recognition, or supportive feedback.

_____ 6. **Assessing and evaluating performance.** In our team, we use quality (comprehensive, valid, reliable, differentiating, useful, and defensible) performance data, compare it with plans, and consider circumstances and challenges to produce fair and objective evaluations.

_____ 7. **Rewarding and recognizing performance.** In our team, all team members and the team leader are fairly rewarded and well recognized for the contributions we make.

_____ **Total**

INTERPRETING YOUR SCORES

0 to 7: Your team probably has little performance management. If you are lucky and have a highly committed group of individuals, it might be successful, but probably not through design. Individuals may be working to different priorities. Some may be focused purely on outputs, but they are damaging team processes; others may be making performance judgments based on incomplete evidence.

8 to 14: Your team has some of the core processes in place, but they are probably somewhat mechanistic rather than enthusiastically applied. Performance management in your team may be more about control and compliance than about engagement and motivation.

15 to 21: Your team is well on the way to having what it takes to truly excel—to be that SuperTeam.

ASSESSMENT REFLECTION EXERCISE

The observation that things have a natural tendency to degenerate has driven researchers, theorists, and pragmatists to struggle for decades to find the magic formula for maximizing performance management. Virtually every year some new management fad is taken up by HR professionals and propagated across their organizations, only to be superseded by the next "hot" model.

However, the RESPECT Model is grounded in robust principles that have stood the test of time. These can be applied to teams as well as individuals, which leads to enhanced and sustained team performance. It is only how they are applied to each individual that changes. Go back and look at your scores for each question:

1. Which one did you find the most difficult to score? Why is this? Is this an aspect of performance that you need to know more about in terms of what "excelling" looks like? Or is this an area that you need to know more about in terms of what happens in your team?

2. Did you score any one section lower than all the others? Why was that? Make a mental note to look out for ideas as you read through this chapter.

Driving Team Performance

While most of us dislike change, we also know that if things remain static, they become stagnant, and performance deteriorates. So change of some sort is a critically important component of sustained or improved performance. The most well-known evidence for the positive impact of change comes from studies conducted by Elton Mayo at the Western Electric Hawthorne Works facility outside of Chicago, Illinois, from 1927 to 1932. In the 1950s, Henry Landsberger analyzed this data and coined the term the Hawthorne effect. Since that time, human resources departments have generated streams of initiatives and new ways of doing things merely to seize upon the positive impacts of giving employees attention from management and instituting change.

Unfortunately, not all of the changes resulted in the sought-after positive impacts, and the means have almost become the ends. This has been especially true in the world of performance management, where changing the forms, the rating scales, and the software programs every few years or even every year has become the norm. Simplicity (usually over effectiveness) has now become the goal!

Last year, an international manufacturing company launched a collaboration and team-working initiative. Extensive investment was made in social media tools for collaborating, sharing documents, generating ideas, and so on. Less than a month later, a new variable compensation scheme was launched to reward individuals based on their individual achievements.

The company claimed, "We are continuing to build a performance culture in which those who contribute the most are rewarded accordingly," and it said that the new scheme would incentivize greater individual performance. It certainly triggered behavior changes, but not the ones that were expected. The impact was virtually immediate. Individuals started to refuse to help one another so that they could focus on achieving their own goals; work for others was done after their own work, rather than at the best time; and so on.

Even simplified annual goal setting does not, and will not, lead to sustained performance improvement. (All top performers have goals, but not all of those with goals are top performers!) Similarly, annual performance appraisal does not, and will not, lead to sustained performance improvement. And trivializing a process so much that we can justify demanding that the poor managers comply with it, while creating something that the good managers know is facile, has little added value either. Similarly, so-called incentive schemes have been proven, with a few exceptions, not to produce the targeted performance improvements. You only have to read Paul's last book, *Carrots and Sticks Don't Work*, or to watch Dan Pink's TED Talk on motivation to understand that. As Dan says, "Businesses don't do what science knows."

However, the fact remains that change does have the potential to trigger new behaviors, and we are seeing a resurgence of interest in the concept of behavior engineering. But we want to focus specifically on performance in teams and how, having established a team, you can ensure that it excels rather than merely performs.

Last year, Clinton became aware of a major bank that invested in developing and communicating a new set of values. One of these was "respect for the employee"—to encourage the employees to be creative and bring innovation to the company. On the same day that the values were announced, HR sent around an e-mail reminding all staff that the use of social media during working time, even on personal devices, was not allowed.

Not only did this new rule trigger the obvious and cynical restroom discussions about whether or not managers knew what they were doing (trust was reduced), it also focused a spotlight on the HR department's failure to spot such an obvious disconnect (respect was reduced).

So, "How do we drive up team performance?" This question isn't just for team leaders. All performance management systems have each of the components shown in Figure 16.1, and in most teams, the team members can have as great an impact on collective performance, by influencing the effectiveness of each component, as the team leader can.

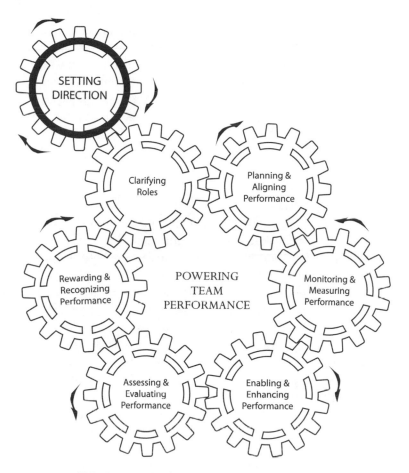

FIGURE 16.1 Performance Management System

In the mid-1980s Clinton was asked to lead a project with 3M United Kingdom as part of a global initiative to enhance the company's performance management processes. During the research for that project, he discovered Pilat HR Solutions.

After he left 3M, he later joined Pilat. Since then, Clinton has developed a passion for how organizations create cultures and processes that maximize individual and collective performance and that encourage and enable individuals and teams to develop to their true potential.

He has led Pilat's research into performance management. One finding has been that, irrespective of the appraisal form, the rating scale, or whether or not performance management is driven by the employee or the manager, all processes have a number of recurring components—the ones shown in Figure 16.1. These exist whether or not they are designed. It's just that what exists may not be what you would prefer!

Setting Direction

Optimum performance can be achieved only if each team member knows what the team is aiming to achieve and how it fits into the greater whole. Only then can the team members believe in the goal and be expected to commit to it.

Setting direction is the process whereby higher-level goals are communicated down through the organization. At the highest level, they comprise the organization's overarching vision, mission, and values. As they cascade through the organization, they form the divisional plans, departmental plans, and corporate initiatives. At the team level, they are "what our team is expected to achieve."

In ineffective organizations, direction setting still occurs. However, it lacks coordination; individual units "do their own thing"; there is little partnering (often departments fight and compete with each other); and expectations are disjointed at best, unclear or undefined at worst.

Organizations that follow the RESPECT Model do the following:

1. The various companies, divisions, regions, functions, departments, and teams, through their leaders, *partner* with each other to achieve alignment of their goals and plans and the like, across the organization as well as up and down.

2. Individual teams in turn are *empowered* to plan how they will make their required contributions to the whole (the outputs and results they will achieve, how they will go about it, and the growth they will invest in for the future). They are also *empowered* to communicate the direction down through their organization, and they are *trusted* to do so appropriately. They own their performance.

3. Leaders *partner* with their team members to help them to understand and respect what the team is required to achieve.
4. The specific *expectations* are made clear, often in SMART (specific, measurable, attainable, relevant, and time bound) objectives, at all levels. They are not trivial expectations— S = specific, not simplistic.

These actions will ensure that individuals have respect for the organization and its leadership.

Clarifying Roles

If two men on the same job agree all the time, then one is useless.
If they disagree all the time, both are useless.

—Darryl F. Zanuck

Clarifying roles takes two forms—clarifying the individuals' roles in terms of the day-to-day work of the team, and clarifying their roles in ensuring that the whole team works well and produces what is expected. Achieving this clarity usually demands that they know all of the other roles within the team and how they interconnect.

In ineffective organizations and teams, roles might be clear but often aren't, and they frequently do not clearly interconnect or reflect the changing demands. In ineffective teams, individuals may care about their own performance but not about their peers' performance.

Organizations that follow the RESPECT Model do the following:

1. Individual and team *expectations* are kept up-to-date 24/7 through dialogue between the leader and the team members.
2. Individuals are *empowered* through their roles to make clear and specific contributions.
3. Individuals understand when and how they are expected to provide each other with *supportive* feedback to ensure excellent team performance.

This ensures that team members have respect for the leader and how their own contributions impact the higher level goals.

Planning and Aligning Performance

Life is about being made to do things you don't want to do and then being glad you were made to, afterward.

—John Garnett

Improved direction setting and clarifying roles increase the chance that team members understand the bigger picture and the relative priorities.

Planning and aligning performance is the process by which the team ensures that all team members know and understand precisely:

- What they are expected to produce—their individual results, outputs, and/or contributions to the team's success.
- How they are expected to do so—tasks, processes, skills to use, behaviors to display, and values to live. We have known for years that exhorting people simply through goal setting to produce more has limited effect on the actual results, and it can even produce negative effects! We have to attend to the question: How are they to meet those expectations?
- Growth or development that is expected so that they can maximize their chance of delivering on their goals and being equipped to take on new challenges.

In ineffective organizations, infrequent planning processes trivialize the *expectations* of individuals and teams. Infrequent reviews that are supposed to track progress and update plans are used merely to remind people of what they agreed to and for those people to perfect their excuses for not having succeeded!

Organizations that follow the RESPECT Model do the following:

1. Team members are *empowered* to develop and maintain their own plans based on what they learned through *setting direction* and *clarifying roles*.
2. Team members are given *supportive feedback* on prior achievements, and they are given help in crafting clear *expectations* in terms of what they will achieve (output), how they will do so (tasks and behaviors), and how they will develop so they can handle greater challenges later (growth).
3. Leaders *partner* with their team members to refine these plans—they view this as a critical part of their job, not just an add-on to it. Team members *partner* with each other to ensure that their respective plans gel.
4. Leaders *trust* their team members to create challenging plans for themselves and to commit to enhancing their performance and the performance of the team . . . until the leaders have reason not to trust them.

This ensures that team members have respect for one another and what they each contribute.

Monitoring and Measuring Performance

When a great team loses through complacency, it will constantly search for new and more intricate explanations to explain away defeat.

—*Pat Riley*

We know that behavior engineering (and this is one goal of performance management) requires frequent triggers and reminders to ensure that new actions are taken. Contemporary technology can trigger desired behaviors by sending e-mails and exception reports based on multiple criteria—for example, set up review, interim, and end dates, keep track of changes made by team members, or set up regular reviews. It can also enable individuals to record ongoing progress notes to avoid the typical "What did I do in February and March?" questions at the end of the year. Having a cumulative record of performance information is crucial for later valid and reliable assessments, as well as for reflective learning and performance redirection.

In ineffective organizations, monitoring and measuring is sparse and considered overly complex. Simplicity rules.

Organizations that follow the RESPECT Model do the following:

1. Team members are *empowered* and equipped to monitor and measure their own performance and the performance of those who serve them.
2. Team members *partner* to ensure that they all know if performance is on track. They don't hide performance from one another.
3. Team members provide real-time *supportive feedback* to one another on progress, shortfalls, and successes.

In this component, *expectations* are monitored, and *trust* in the team is sustained by ensuring real-time and objective evidence of progress and achievements. This provides the evidence base from which individual team members can respect their fellow team members and the team as a whole.

Enabling and Enhancing Performance

Amy was made redundant from her market researcher position. She struggled to find a new role, but eventually she found one as a director's personal assistant (PA). Prospects looked good, and things initially went well. However, after making a series of mistakes including sending a director to a client over 400 miles from the office on the wrong day, she found herself on a written warning.

"I'm sorry. She has to go. This makes no sense. I have to check everything she does multiple times. I don't have a PA. I have a personal Pain in the A$S!"

"I agree, but it makes no sense. She must be able to be extremely accurate and fast. She's not stupid."

"Well, you take her then. Put her in your analytics team. See where she gets you."

"OK."

* * *

"Well, how did it go then? Do we still have any clients after Amy's creative analytics?"

"Actually, it is going really well. We are ahead this month; two clients have commissioned new work; and Amy has developed some really innovative ways of handling the reporting."

The turnaround was not magic. It was relatively simple. Amy's earlier poor performance was caused by her boss's micromanaging (which undermined her confidence, already damaged by her redundancy), by her fear of failure (triggered by the director's sarcastic personal style), and by her being treated as a servant rather than as a valued assistant who was providing an important service. A little *respect, supportive feedback*, and *trust* had a major positive impact.

Enabling and enhancing performance is the driver of change and the sustainer of maximum performance. It is sometimes quoted that:

Performance = capability × opportunity × inclination

There is a lot of truth in that, and we add one further component, **awareness**:

Performance = capability × opportunity × inclination × awareness

So, enabling and enhancing performance is about addressing the four elements of performance:

1. Capability. To increase capability, we must enable the team members to acquire any needed knowledge and skills, *empower* and *trust* them with the chance to practice, coach and provide *supportive feedback* to redirect, and most of all *recognize* successes to reinforce individual elements of excellent performance.

2. Opportunity. Individuals can excel only if they are given the chance to do so (including the chance to fail). This demands *empowering* them to make noncritical mistakes and *trusting* them to learn from them . . . until proven wrong!

3. Inclination. Inclination is largely self-generated, but team members and team leaders can help by bringing the future alive, demonstrating commitment to the goals, providing *supportive feedback* and *recognition* . . . oh, and avoiding demotivating one another!

4. Awareness. Typically, underperforming employees do not believe that they are—in self-appraisals and surveys, over 80 percent of employees have been found to rate themselves as "above average"! This lack of self-awareness can be addressed only through *supportive feedback*—face-to-face, or at least in real time. Evidence-based feedback and planning reviews are crucially important.

In ineffective organizations, performance reviews are formal, rare, and intermittent; they are add-ons to the job. Reliance is placed on the talent of the individuals, not on the interactions between them. Enhanced performance is expected to come through a combination of control, process, and financial incentives.

Organizations that follow the RESPECT Model do the following:

1. Team leaders are *expected* to optimize the performance of their team members and the team as a whole. They are held accountable for how they deal with the team, not merely for the results.
2. Team leaders ensure that individuals are capable and equipped and that they have the opportunity to excel. They *partner* with each team member to enable success.
3. Team leaders do all they can to maximize team member self-awareness, motivation, and repeated success through *supportive feedback*, *trust*, and *recognition*.

Assessing and Evaluating Performance

When there is objective evidence of performance against expectations, an assessment and evaluation can be made. This component acknowledges that unexpected demands and circumstances may have significantly helped or hindered performance, and it enables us, more objectively, to convert "Did we or did we not achieve our goals [objective fact/assessment]?" into "Did we perform well or poorly [evaluation]?"

This is one component where showing *consideration* (for the changing demands and circumstances) and building *trust* (in the process of assessment) are keys to future performance. All too often performance appraisals merely flatter the good performers and demotivate the very employees whose performance we seek to enhance.

In ineffective organizations, performance appraisal is trivialized into an annual event when individuals are lumped into boxes through indefensible so-called *calibration exercises* (meetings in which preconceived prejudices and opinions are reinforced with dubious anecdotes from the ill-informed!).

Organizations that follow the RESPECT Model do the following:

1. Performance appraisal is a cumulative process throughout the period, continuously informed by *supportive feedback*.
2. Team members are *trusted* to accumulate a portfolio of evidence of performance against expectations, and the expectations were developed through partnering to meet changing demands and circumstances.
3. Team members are *recognized* for successes and encouraged to repeat them. *Consideration* is given for circumstances beyond their control.

This component should achieve clarity and understanding of each individual's performance and the performance of the team as a whole, and it should build the employees' *trust* in the leader and the process.

Rewarding and Recognizing Performance

Most individuals' minds become more focused on issues when the importance of the issues is underpinned by consequences and benefits. However, far fewer people than performance management process designs would suggest are motivated primarily by money. Yet, most organizations still place substantial importance on the connection between performance and pay, and they continuously grapple with the balance between individual and team payments.

The evidence is clear and building that the following is true:

1. "Carrots and Sticks Don't Work" in most situations, and they certainly don't work in those situations in which performance demands are likely to change, and in which creativity and individual accountability are needed.
2. Employee engagement (the desire to give maximum discretionary performance and to stick with the task even through the tough times) is impacted far more by the RESPECT drivers, especially *recognition*, *empowerment*, and *supportive feedback*, than by any financial mechanisms—as long as a sufficient level of pay is already in place.

On Your Playing Field

Think about what you have learned in this chapter, about how it relates to your team, and how it relates to each team member. Think about how your performance management process operates and select one or two elements that you can enhance through conscious application of the RESPECT Model.

SETTING DIRECTION Improving the extent to which the team as a whole and each team member has a clear and specific understanding of higher-level goals, plans, and organizational values. We know and understand the priorities, and we know how we are expected to operate.

CLARIFYING ROLES Making sure that all team members clearly understand their roles in terms of (a) the specific job as well as (b) the roles they are expected to play in the performance of the team as a whole. We *partner*, and we clarify *expectations*.

PLANNING AND ALIGNING PERFORMANCE Creating and maintaining comprehensive individual performance plans (for the what, how, and development), tightly aligned to maximize our collective performance.

MONITORING AND MEASURING PERFORMANCE Ensuring that we track progress and produce meaningful data on which to base change. We continuously monitor results, tasks and behaviors, and the development needed, taking into account incoming *supportive feedback*.

ENABLING AND ENHANCING PERFORMANCE Focusing on improving performance through capability, opportunities, and increasing inclination.

ASSESSING AND EVALUATING PERFORMANCE Using only quality (comprehensive, valid, reliable, differentiating, useful, and defensible) performance data to determine fair and objective evaluations.

REWARDING AND RECOGNIZING PERFORMANCE Applying the RESPECT Model to ensure the motivation of our team leader and team members.

Wrap-Up

In order to achieve sound team performance, conventional wisdom still applies. We need clear goals, leadership, skills, and effective processes and communications.

In order to achieve SuperTeam performance, we need to examine the components of the performance management system and how we can apply the RESPECT Model to each of them.

Up Next

Even with the best will in the world, an excellent group of candidates, and a robust selection and onboarding process, we can still end up with team members who no longer fit the team and even a whole team that is no longer needed.

In the next chapter, we examine exiting team members.

CHAPTER 17 # Exiting Team Members

In the minds of great managers, consistent poor performance is not primarily a matter of weakness, stupidity, disobedience, or disrespect. It is a matter of miscasting.

—*Marcus Buckingham*

Overview

People come and go—it's a reality, but it can be renewing. Sometimes turnover in a team is voluntary, and sometimes it is forced. Sometimes it is desirable—for example, the individual did not fit into the team, or there was insufficient work. Sometimes it is undesirable—for example, individuals have been poached by another team or organization, or they simply didn't like the job despite being good at it.

In this chapter, we explore how best to handle departures respectfully so that maximum ongoing performance and minimum undesirable future attrition are achieved. We explore exiting team members and disbanding entire teams.

SUPERSTARTER QUESTIONS

1. Think of a time when a team member left your team. How do you think the person felt after the experience?

2. How do you think the person felt about the team after the experience?
3. Based on that person's experience, how might she have helped or damaged the team after she left?
4. How did you and the other team members feel immediately after she left?
5. Under what circumstances should you consider exiting all of the team members—that is, disbanding your entire team?

TEAM ASSESSMENT

Instructions: Read each statement below, and, using the following scale, decide how accurately it describes your team:

Strongly disagree: 0 points
Disagree: 1 point
Agree: 2 points
Strongly agree: 3 points

Place the point value of your answer choice on the blank line at the beginning of each of the following statements:

_____ 1. **Team members take the initiative to express any dissatisfaction with being on the team.**

_____ 2. **Supportive action is taken as soon as it is clear that someone is not delivering what is expected of him. We set people up to succeed.**

_____ 3. **We take action to help people leave if they can't or don't want to fit in.**

_____ 4. **We strategically review the need for the team and in what form, if at all, it should continue.**

_____ 5. **We take action when someone leaves the team, to learn why that happened, address any issues, and to do better in the future.**

_____ **Total score**

INTERPRETING YOUR SCORES

0 to 5: People leaving your team or staying when that may not be in the team's best interests may be having an avoidable negative impact on the team. Think about why people are exiting and how those departures are being handled because there is need for improvement. Consider whether it would be best for the team to disband.

6 to 10: Your team is well on the way to handling the issue of exiting. However, there is still room for improvement. You may still have people on the team that you shouldn't have, or you may not be handling departures as well as you could. This could be adversely impacting the team, and it may even be contributing to future attrition. Make sure that you are keeping the team relevant.

11 to 15: Your team seems to manage team member departure effectively, and you are either at SuperTeam status or well on the way. Continue to focus on refining the team. Ensure that the team continues to add value to the organization and each team member continues to add value to the team.

ASSESSMENT REFLECTION EXERCISE

By the time people actually leave a team, a company, or a relationship, it is typically already six months since they decided that they needed to go or the organization decided that they should go. At any point in time, you could have people on your team (you could even be one of them) who have been mentally and emotionally disconnected for months—coming in, living the title, taking the pay, but disengaged from the work, their colleagues, and the organization. In a SuperTeam, both the number of such occurrences and the timelines of each occurrence are kept to a minimum.

1. What has your experience told you about what really matters when people exit a team?
2. In your team, do team members who are not fully committed come out and say so?
3. If they do, are they actively supported by the team to make a next successful move?

4. Are team members who do not fit, for whatever reason, provided with supportive feedback and helped to change, or are they exited?
5. Are teams that are no longer needed ever disbanded?

Why People Leave Teams

Here are 10 common reasons why team members choose, of their own volition, to leave teams. Identify any that you believe may apply to current team members, and note what you can do, if anything, to address the situation **if you want to**:

_____ **1.** The role does not use their knowledge and skills, they do not feel well utilized, or they do not feel challenged.
_____ **2.** They do not believe in the goals of the team.
_____ **3.** They do not feel they know or understand what is expected of them.
_____ **4.** They do not know where they stand. They do not receive feedback on their performance.
_____ **5.** They do not have a good working relationship with their fellow team members.
_____ **6.** They do not have a good working relationship with the team leader.
_____ **7.** They do not have the skills to be successful in their job.
_____ **8.** They see no opportunities for personal development or career progression.
_____ **9.** They do not feel respected or trusted.
_____ **10.** Others are trying to poach them by making enticing propositions.

Handling Resignations from the Team Disrespectfully

Here are some ways that teams handle resignations _disrespectfully_:

1. Even if the news is welcome, flatter the individuals who are resigning, and tell them how much they will be missed.
2. Say nothing other than, "OK. When do you want to leave?"
3. Tell them that they have made a mistake.
4. Ask them immediately if they would assist in the future if urgently needed.
5. Escort them to their workstation to clear out their personal property, and immediately demand the credit cards and keys, turn off their e-mail, and so on.

Reflect on any situations where you have had resignations from a team. Has the team fallen foul of any of the above?

Handling Resignations from the Team with RESPECT

Here are some ways that SuperTeams handle resignations using the RESPECT Model. *Note:* In SuperTeams, we do not believe that you should try to convince individuals to stay when they have already gotten to the point of actually leaving—the point at which they are ready to go is way beyond the time when they first started considering it!

1. Ask them what you or other team members did to contribute to their decision, and listen to learn.
2. Ask them what you or other team members could have done to produce a different conclusion, and listen to learn.
3. Offer to *partner* with them and provide *supportive feedback* to handle their exit in a way that is good for you and good for them.
4. Ask them what you could do going forward to strengthen the team and to reduce such attrition.
5. Make clear your *expectations* of them while they are still in the role in terms of their work, their relations with their clients, team leader, and team members, and their network of role-related contacts.

6. Tell all the other team members at the same time. Don't focus on any negatives in the individual who is leaving. Focus on what you expect from the rest of the team in relation to the individual who is leaving.

Why You May Want People to Leave the Team

Bad attitudes will ruin your team.

—*Terry Bradshaw*

Here are 10 reasons why you should consider exiting team members. Check any that you believe apply to current team members:

_____ **1.** They evidently do not want to be part of the team.

_____ **2.** They cannot or will not produce the output expected.

_____ **3.** They cannot or will not perform the tasks expected in the required manner.

_____ **4.** They cannot or will not acquire the knowledge and skills needed now and/or for the future.

_____ **5.** They do not fit with the team—there is a clash of values.

_____ **6.** Their attitude and actions negatively impact the performance of others.

_____ **7.** They undermine other team members.

_____ **8.** They do nothing to help other team members to excel.

_____ **9.** They take the credit for work done by others.

_____ **10.** There is clear evidence that they cannot be trusted.

If there are underperformers in your team, all the other team members are likely to be watching and asking, "Why doesn't somebody fix this?" In SuperTeams, even mediocre performance by a single member is unacceptable. In SuperTeams, prompt action is taken. In

SuperTeams, somebody *does* fix it—and not always the team leader. Are you putting off addressing a performance or a fit issue?

Exiting Team Members Disrespectfully

Here are some ways that teams encourage people to leave or they exit people *disrespectfully*:

1. Spread rumors that they are not performing well and hope that they leave of their own volition.
2. Withhold promotions and/or opportunities that they could reasonably expect.
3. Ostracize them by leaving them out of important events and meetings. Don't keep them informed about team matters.
4. Allow or even encourage others to do what they should be doing—informally replace them.
5. Time the exiting badly—for example, just after you know they have taken out a major loan or on the first shift of the week.

Reflect on the preceding list. Have you done or are you doing any of these? Have any of these things happened to you? If so, think about how you can handle the situation more respectfully and why you should do so.

Exiting Team Members with RESPECT

Here are some ways that SuperTeams exit people using the RESPECT Model. It is critical to understand that the rest of the team is watching how this process is being handled. Your application of these steps may vary if the individuals are staying in the organization—that is, they are merely leaving your team:

1. Provide them with robust *supportive feedback*, and offer to *partner* with them to avoid the need for them to exit.
2. Have a witness with you when you tell them (this will usually be someone with HR expertise and never another team member) to make sure that the dialogue is clear and effective.

3. Show *consideration* by asking them how they would like their colleagues to be informed. (You don't have to agree to all their requests, but you are better off knowing their preferences.)

4. Show *consideration* by telling them on the last working shift of the week. That will give them a chance to compose themselves before meeting their colleagues again the next week (if they have to).

5. Show *consideration* by offering them the chance to leave immediately or later if that is a permissible option, and give them some privacy (without risking security) to cope with the news.

6. Tell them clearly and concisely that they are being exited; this is not the time for a discussion of the evidence and explanations. This action should not be a total surprise (except in critical immediate termination situations).

7. Provide them immediately with all the information and documents they need—for example, medical insurance information, benefits advice, final payment, and access to career counseling or outplacement services if appropriate. *Empower* them to take control so they can rebuild their career.

8. Complete in a dignified way all of the procedural and legal actions necessary—for example, get back credit cards, passes, keys, and equipment; and disable security passes, e-mail, and voice mail. Make all *expectations* of them clear—for example, give them whatever information they might need about their NDAs and any other post-termination obligations they might have.

9. *Partner* with them in advising people, especially their network of contacts, that they are leaving the team or the organization. Focus on providing nonjudgmental explanations and new contact details as appropriate.

10. Don't burn bridges. There are always three sides to every story—yours, theirs, and the truth! In that context, bad-mouthing and spreading rumors about exiting team members has never helped anyone, and they have an amazing habit of backfiring.

Ensure, as much as you can, that the person does not leave feeling angry, slighted, bitter, or upset. Sometimes that is not possible, but it is important to minimize any negative feelings.

After People Have Gone

Whenever people leave, for good or bad reasons, here are things you should do to ensure SuperTeam status.

Learn from the Experience

1. Partner with the team to diagnose why you ended up with people you did not want on the team or people who did not want to be on the team. Something went wrong.
2. If people leave of their own volition, they usually tell you why they are going to the new role—for example, it offers more pay or better opportunities, or it requires less travel. But that is often not why they first started thinking of leaving. More likely, they did not like the work, their peers were annoying, they did not like their boss, or the job was not what they expected. You must try to uncover what made them switch, one day, from ignoring other opportunities to actively taking notice.
3. You need to understand why one or more of your processes failed: (a) the selection process, (b) the onboarding process, and/or (c) the performance management process—especially if you have terminated team members.

Know Your Current Team

Take steps to know your team. This requires ruthless attention to understanding the individual hearts and minds of your team members whether you are the team leader or not. What energizes them? What demotivates them? What do they like doing? What do they do well? What do they not like doing? What do they do poorly?

Don't Make Excuses for Poor Performance

SuperTeams do not tolerate poor performance. They enhance it. SuperTeams do not tolerate poor performers. They grow or replace them. SuperTeams do not rationalize why team members underperform. They get to the true cause and do something about it.

Invest in the Future

Every time team members exit, it is a chance to send messages to the team members who are staying:

1. Demonstrate sincere recognition by explaining to existing team members the things that the departing team members did that were good . . . people rarely fail to make any meaningful contributions.
2. Reaffirm empowerment so that team members know and understand the implications of the other people leaving. For example, what are they empowered to do pending the replacement of the departing team members?
3. Provide supportive feedback, particularly if they have been helpful in managing the departure and picking up important decisions or work.
4. Clarify expectations. This is a chance to ensure that they all know what is expected of them to ensure that they are not next!
5. Reinforce trust by being clear and transparent about what happened and why within the limits that confidentiality allows.

Sustain Networks

SuperTeam members invest in building their networks. The minute people leave your team, those networks are potentially lost:

1. As a team, invest in sharing your contacts and keeping them up-to-date while people are still with you. You never know when you may need the contacts.
2. When people exit, as quickly as possible identify their contacts—for example, through e-mail, phone, and text-messaging trails—and make new contacts or reinforce other existing team contacts with them.

Look After Yourself and the Other Remaining Team Members

During difficult times, and especially when we lose critical people out of our teams, it gets stressful. Consider the following simple ways to look after yourself better, and advise other team members to do the same:

1. Exercise (subject to advice from your doctor if appropriate), and eat well (based on sound and appropriate advice rather than based on populist diet fads and vendors trying to sell you something). Respect your body—you only get one!
2. Learn to relax, sleep enough, and get some humor into your life. Respect your brain—you only get one!
3. Make time to do things you like to do, and savor them. Respect your time and that of others—we all get the same; it's only how we use it that varies.
4. Keep a journal. Many people find journaling therapeutic, and there is evidence that doing so helps people through the most horrendous experiences of being hostages, prisoners, depressives, and so on. So it should help with the stress that may be associated with the departure of a team member.
5. And the best advice of all: suck it up! Some things are just the way they have to be. You can choose how you feel. Simply deciding to accept certain things as they are and moving on can ease the burden.

Disbanding the Entire Team

Unfortunately, it is much easier to create a team than it is to disband one.

Why Disband an Entire Team?

One of the ways to enhance the quality of teamwork in an organization is to ensure that the teamwork is truly valued—that is, when teams are effective, their work adds value and they are appreciated; when teams are not effective, they are disbanded! We cannot tell you whether your team should be nurtured, pruned, or euthanized! That has to be your decision. However, here are some considerations:

1. Is the goal still valid that the team was originally set up to achieve?
2. Does the work required to achieve that goal still need collective effort, or could it be achieved just as effectively or better by individuals?
3. Is that collective effort such that the people who exert it need to be part of the same group, or could their efforts be commissioned on demand, as needed?
4. Can the goals be achieved by another and more effective or more efficient means?
5. Do you have a set of criteria that you can use to determine whether the team should be disbanded or not?
6. Do people ask to join your team? If they do, it indicates that the work of your team is respected and valued by others in the organization.

How Do You Disband an Entire Team?

Here are some thoughts that you may be able to modify to suit your specific circumstances.

As you will assume by now, disbanding an entire team should be executed with RESPECT. Show *respect* for the team by actively involving them in the disbanding process. This can be difficult if, as a result, some may lose their jobs, which in some states and countries, could trigger legal processes. However, within the limitations of what you are allowed to do, actively involving the team in a positive process is far better than dealing a destructive blow. Ineffective processes create fear and confusion; they leave team members feeling slighted, alone, and resentful. They leave those who dealt with the team embarrassed, concerned, and unsupported. All of these feelings can adversely affect other people in the organization.

Create a systematic and transparent process that looks after the business and the team members. Communicate clearly, honestly, and factually. Explain briefly why. And also explain fully what, how, and when.

Our initial feelings when our teams are disbanded are not unlike those associated with grieving. A number of models of the stages people go through when grieving have been adapted for non-life and death situations. Most models are similar to the more common shock, anger, rejection, acceptance (SARA) change management model. Here we present our own team disbanding model—stages through which the team members will go and ideas for how you can handle them.

Stage 1: Shock and Denial. *"OMG! This cannot be happening! What do you mean you are disbanding the team? We are blitzed with meetings and reports that have to get done."*

Shock is almost inevitable when an entire team is to be disbanded. In fact, a natural reaction to sudden change can even be to deny that it is actually going to happen. "We're fine—honestly. We can get through this. You need us." These reactions are defense mechanisms, and some people can get locked into this stage. Assuming that the decision to disband the team is final, it is very important to be clear with people: "Yes, the team is being disbanded by [date]." Do not give any indication that there is ambiguity about the decision because providing false hope is disrespectful.

Stage 2: Anger. Typically, shock and denial rapidly turn into anger. *"They are disbanding us because of what? How dare they? If it weren't for us, they would be in deep doo-doo. Is that all the thanks that we get for all those weekends and vacations when we came in! I'll let them have a piece of my mind when they come and see us . . . if they do!"*

Anger is cumulative and corrosive. Anger has to be dissipated. Within reason, do not deny the team members the opportunity to vent. However, seek to contain it so that it does not adversely affect others in the organization. Take steps to avoid escalation. As the saying goes, "Someone told me that, if I think about it, things could be worse. I did! And they are!" Listen attentively to the team members, and identify the best time to attempt to refocus the energy on moving forward.

Stage 3: Negotiating. In this stage, the team calms down and seeks to delay or divert the consequences: "What if we offered to share some of the work. Perhaps we could keep a small subteam."

If the decision is final, it is unwise to say things like, "OK. Leave it with me, and I will see what I can do."

However, there may be opportunities to review other roles and to allow team members to debate and agree on their personal terms and times of departure. Allowing some to assist in closing down can also be therapeutic. Focus discussions and activities only on those things that can be influenced or changed.

Stage 4: Demotivated and Lonely. This is the stage when reality strikes! It is typically characterized by cynicism, sluggishness, and a feeling of being excluded. "Why should I bother now?" But even if the team's work is to be ceased, there are usually many loose ends that need to be tidied up. So at the very point in time when the team needs to be very effective, the team members are likely to be in this stage, making the team its most dysfunctional. You need the team to get through this stage as quickly as possible.

Avoid sympathy ("I feel the same way")—two depressed people fueling each other is not good. Empathy is more effective ("I understand how you feel; here's my take on what we need to do now"). Get as many of the team members as possible to work together. Pride in a final good job really can be gained.

Stage 5: Capturing Learning. If there is a chance that the team or one similar could be formed again in the future, create a "How-to Guide." Get the team members to contribute to it, perhaps even personal chapters. Make sure that these topics are covered: knowledge and skills needed; types of people; communications; locations; processes; and the style of management and leadership that appear to be most effective.

Help individual team members to learn from their own experiences. Facilitate a session in which team members receive structured feedback from one another on their relative strengths and their relative limitations with respect to team skills. Ensure that each element of feedback is delivered as supportive feedback, showing consideration and giving recognition when possible. Feedback should be supported by evidence and examples, and it should focus on behavior, not on the individuals. Each team member should leave with this knowledge:

1. These are the one or two strengths I brought to the team and can take elsewhere.

2. These are the one or two things I need to learn to do differently to add value to my next team.

Partner with individual team members to capture the learning and benefits to them of having been on the team. Provide them with *supportive feedback* and *recognition*.

Actively encourage and *partner* with them in updating their résumés and sharing their contact lists and personal contact information. Explore what, with the limited time available, the team members can do to help one another by *partnering* on job hunting and knowledge sharing.

If appropriate, work together to prepare for moving to the new roles, new teams, and so on. After all, this may be a rebirth rather than a funeral.

Stage 6: Celebrating Success. Last but not least, celebrate team successes such as these:

1. Achievement of specific team goals
2. Delivery of the team plan
3. The way the team was built and worked together
4. The way the team developed in knowledge and skills
5. The extent to which team members developed
6. The professionalism with which it closed out the work and the team

Success breeds success—so celebrate it.

On Your Playing Field

Think about each team to which you belong or that you lead:

1. What were its goals, and are they still valid?
2. What was its expected life cycle, and is that nearly up?
3. Is collective effort still the best way of achieving current goals?
4. If not, should the team be disbanded? If so, how should that be handled?
5. Assuming the team should continue, who, if anyone, on your team has been considering leaving or has disengaged

from the team? How can you partner with them or provide supportive feedback to recover the situation or enable them to exit with minimum damage to the team?

6. Who, if anyone, on your team is seriously underperforming? Is it time to exit them? If so, when and how are you going to do that?

7. Who on the team needs more attention (recognition, empowerment, supportive feedback, clarification of expectations, consideration, or trust)? What are you going to do to address that to avoid potential exiting?

Wrap-Up

Team member transitions are inevitable and not necessarily negative. In fact, it may be very healthy for both the team and the individual. Disbanding and exiting are processes that are just as important as recruiting, and they need to be mastered.

Applying the RESPECT Model to those who exit as well as to those who stay can dramatically decrease the potential adverse impact of transitions. Those who exit can become your ambassadors. With inadequate respect, they become your public critics. Those who stay watch and learn from how you treat people who need to be exited and those who leave voluntarily—we demonstrate our true beliefs and values when under pressure, not when things are going well.

It is a natural tendency, and it is easy to create a team. We need to think about the criteria by which to disband the team at the time when we create it—it makes the later decision much easier. It is very difficult to create an effective and efficient team; we need to be able to determine when to fix it and when to disband it.

Once formed, teams find useful work to do and create an illusion of still being necessary. Disbanding a team can be a positive process for the team members, the team leader, and the organization. Disbanding teams with RESPECT can be challenging, but if done well, it is energizing.

Look after yourself. Do not be the one who exits because you have failed to attend to your own health, happiness, and ability to be a SuperTeam member. If you have become disengaged, take responsibility to find ways to reengage with your team and its mission.

Up Next

Fortunately, especially in SuperTeams, it is rare that we exit members or disband. We are more commonly faced with the challenge of sustaining and enhancing the performance of the ongoing team.

In the next chapter we explore team rewards and incentives (to complement the recognition that we have addressed in earlier chapters).

CHAPTER 18

Motivating Through Team Rewards, Incentives, and Recognition

There are two things people want more than sex
and money: recognition and praise.

—Mary Kay Ash

Overview

Despite evidence to the contrary, organizations continue to pump funds into incentive schemes without evidence of their effectiveness. Unfortunately, as Dan Pink so eloquently put it in his TED Talk "The Puzzle of Motivation," "Businesses don't do what science knows," and as Paul Marciano put it, "Carrots and Sticks Don't Work."

In Chapter 4 we articulated, as powerfully as we could, the critically important role of *recognition* in driving up engagement, efficiency, effectiveness, and team member retention.

In this chapter, we address the reality that many organizations, maybe yours, will continue to try to use money to achieve a similar effect. We share ideas on how to do the best you can if faced with that demand.

SUPERSTARTER QUESTIONS

1. What motivates your team to work well together?
2. What motivates your team to deliver the best possible results?
3. What motivates you to perform at your best?
4. What demotivates you such that it reduces your willingness and interest in working with others?
5. What demotivates you such that it reduces your output?

TEAM ASSESSMENT

Instructions: Read each statement below, and, using the following scale, decide how accurately it describes your team:

Strongly disagree: 0 points
Disagree: 1 point
Agree: 2 points
Strongly agree: 3 points

Place the point value of your answer choice on the blank line at the beginning of each of the following statements:

____ 1. **Team members are well compensated for their work.**
____ 2. **There is a clear link between individual pay and individual results and output.**
____ 3. **There is a clear link between individual pay and individual capability and effort.**
____ 4. **There is a clear link between individual pay and team achievements.**
____ 5. **Team members are highly motivated by the potential rewards they can receive.**

____ **Total score**

INTERPRETING YOUR SCORES

0 to 5: Pay may be an issue for this team, and it is a subject that can become corrosive if not attended to. Individuals are likely to be feeling unfairly treated, and this needs addressing. Many individuals may have little incentive to enhance their performance.

6 to 10: The basics of a fair pay scheme appear to be in place to ensure that the team feels adequately rewarded. There may be issues related to perceived fairness. You also need to investigate whether any funds being fed into variable compensation are paying back.

11 to 15: Your team appears to have rewarding and incentivizing performance in hand. You may have or you may be close to achieving SuperTeam status. But you are advised to check on whether the processes you have really do work, that is, that they are genuinely resulting in a meaningful, sustained improvement on performance.

ASSESSMENT REFLECTION EXERCISE

In the assessment questionnaire above, we have included the classic assumption that individual team members will be motivated to perform better if they are offered a financial incentive. But incentivizing individual performance is not simple; and incentivizing team performance is substantially more complex. The principles behind both may be simple to articulate (offer a financial reward, link it to an aspect of performance, pay out based on results)—but their application is far more challenging: "The devil is in the details."

Are assumptions about what gets team members motivated valid? If your organization uses any form of incentive scheme, does it understand how it works (if it does), and why? Individuals have individual needs and drivers. How well are these individual needs understood and addressed within your team?

1. Whom within your team would you most like to see more motivated and why—and it may be you?
2. What do you know about this individual's aspirations, needs, and wants? Are those clear, and are they being met?
3. Is a financial incentive going to work for this unmotivated team member?
4. Would that same incentive work for the other team members?
5. If your team is not performing well, is this primarily to do with individual performances or how team members are working with one another?

Some years ago, Clinton worked with a company on the issue of employee engagement. Clinton was speaking with individual employees in one team, trying to get a feel for how well motivated they were. The team had five team members, including two women who had similar educational and professional backgrounds, and had the same job title and responsibilities within the organization. He expected similar responses to his questions. Oh no!

He had a long conversation with the first who described how her manager worked. Each day, he came around and asked how things were going and whether there were any problems, offered advice on any issues, took time to comment on the positive things that had been done since his last walk-around, and made sure to ask if there was anything he could do to help out. She was clearly motivated, she felt respected for what she did, and she respected the manager accordingly.

He then spoke with the second team member—remember: same job, similar personal life situation, similar circumstances, same manager. The result was very interesting.

"He comes around every morning and tells me what a good job I am doing. He doesn't need to tell me. I know! I just want to be left alone to get on with my job and be paid. He must have more important things to do. If he has to do this every day, he should spend more time with [the other team member]. She needs all this flattery. If he wants me to know what a great job I'm doing he can just give me a raise."

Needs, wants, and aspirations are clearly unique to each individual!

Think about what you could do differently to encourage more effective or more efficient teamwork and to build stronger relationships within the team.

Incentives, Rewards, and Recognition

It has been shown time and time again that financial incentives almost never have a long-term positive impact on satisfaction, engagement, or performance and often have a significant negative impact. When they do work, however, they tend to work most effectively in the following circumstances:

1. The work is of a repetitive and prescriptive nature—for example, manufacturing lines, storyboarded call centers, retail checkouts, or commodity services.
2. The work does not require much, if any, mental agility, problem solving, or creativity.
3. The people doing the work have particular personality profiles—for example, they are goal driven, they like risks, they are opportunistic, or they like *things* more than people. Think stockbrokers.

The debate about the efficacy of *performance-related pay* in any form as a motivator is much like politics—individuals approach the subject with fairly hardened predetermined positions, and they listen to others' arguments primarily to spot the flaws in them, not to be educated by them. Often, they are not even arguing about the same thing. So let's first define some terms.

INCENTIVES. This term refers to payments offered in advance of performance—for example, results, output, effort, behavior, or development—specifically to encourage the individuals to produce performance that is not otherwise anticipated. Incentives are therefore investments in anticipated future performance. These are the carrots.

REWARDS. This term refers to payments made following performance, to remunerate the individuals for their achievements and/or efforts. Typically, rewards are financial, but they do not have to be. Many organizations now offer so-called *cafeteria benefits*, where employees can select from a range of benefits that add up to a given total dollar value. These benefits can include health, dental, and eye care, life insurance, cars, gym memberships, vacations, and child care. Rewards can also include ad hoc awards—for example, for special achievements, long service, and so on.

RECOGNITION. This term refers to an acknowledgment to individuals for something they have done or achieved. The recognition may be a thing, such as a plaque, a gift, service, or money, or it may be merely the process of recognition. For example, it might be a mention in the company newsletter, a toast at a dinner, or a meeting agenda item under "all other business" (AOB), or it could even be something said one-to-one. The "feel-good" factor it can produce lays a foundation for future performance.

Exploring Incentives

It's important to understand why some incentive schemes fail while others succeed.

Why Do Incentives Fail?

In his prior book, *Carrots and Sticks Don't Work*, Paul put together such a comprehensive and compelling list of reasons against the use of traditional individual reward and recognition programs that their use can no longer be justified. In summary, the evidence against the use of extrinsic rewards to motivate employees has been around for many years; far from producing net returns on investment, they often lead to a decrease in morale and productivity.

Aren't Team Incentives the Answer?

Many argue that team incentives are the answer, but this is evidently not the case. In many cases in which team incentives have been applied, the relatively poor performers (at whom presumably incentives are aimed!) don't expect to get paid the incentive, so they perform normally and are carried by the top performers (who become demotivated by having to do so). Or if the awards are paid based solely on team performance, the top performers soon get tired of funding the mediocre and poor performers.

Primarily, these schemes fail because they focus on outcomes, not on engineering the specific behaviors and processes that lead to excellent results.

Why Do Organizations Keep Designing Incentive Schemes That Will Fail?

There appear to be three major reasons.

The first is that most of us have been educated and now work in a capitalist society (even if we work for not-for-profit or government organizations) in which money is the primary measure of success. That perception even pervades our entertainment—game shows like *The Apprentice*, *Dragon's Den*, and *The Price Is Right*. Intuitively, therefore, money must work as a motivator, right?

All compensation professionals with whom Clinton has spoken about financial incentives have given similar explanations abut how those schemes must work, for example, "Take last year. Our top 10 percent of performers earned 50 percent of the incentive pot, or 95 percent of those getting the top bonuses are in our high-potential list." Well, of course they are—it would be a seriously questionable scheme, wouldn't it, if it paid out mainly to poor performers . . . or, wait a minute . . . wasn't that the idea, to incentivize the poor performers to get better? Shouldn't the poor performers who have improved be getting the big-bucks awards?

The second reason organizations keep designing incentive schemes that don't work is that, occasionally and with certain types of employees, they DO work, and we cling to individual anecdotes even if they are not representative. Incentivized manufacturing processes have existed since well before the industrial revolution. Some even claim that the term *piecework* (that is, paying for the production of each "piece" to incentivize rapid, quality work) was derived from the early masonic guilds. Master stone crafters assigned "pieces" of work to apprentices who were paid only when suitable work was produced—in those days, with no social benefits, needing money merely to eat was sufficient motivation to perform. Even today, in many of our telesales and call centers, the processes and philosophies are not much different.

In a similar vein, many sales processes are dependent on commissions, one of the purest forms of incentivized performance-related pay scales. However, it has been repeatedly shown that you have to be a special sort of person to want to be and to be effective in a sales role. This work is not for everyone; in fact, it is a good fit for a very small percentage of the population. It has also been shown that sales incentives, when they work, can often produce very undesirable side effects. Ever attend a session involving sales of time-share properties?

Peter was the consummate salesman dealing in commercial photo-copiers. It was soon after the market had kicked off, so the territory was fertile. He had a great sales territory in which to sell—an area packed with small, highly competitive businesses, most run by their founder-owners who took great pride in being just that little bit better than their next-door neighbors.

Peter's approach was simple. First, qualify them—that is, determine that they could make sensible use of a copier. Next, demonstrate an entry-level machine suited to their needs. Then bring the future alive with some stories about how much easier their administration would be with the help of the copier. Finally, close the deal. So, what is the problem?

Peter was on a commission scheme that already assumed that he sold a significant number of these relatively cheap (he'd say, "very inexpensive") machines. It was going to be a real challenge to increase his commission significantly just by selling these. He was also locked into a team bonus that, because many of the team members were rookies, he could not see them achieving. Therefore, his potential earnings were limited since part of them was out of his control and in jeopardy.

He had to do something more. Help the team members? No—why would he do that? The potential for return was small.

No, it had to be Plan B! On his next call, just as he was going to the van to get the desktop copier for the new client, he turned back and said, "I think you have made the correct decision. Your next-door neighbor has just ordered the CX56—that's definitely too big for your business."

"The CX56? You didn't show me that one."

"Correct. I think the small one is ideal for what you need. Your neighbor probably has a higher volume."

"Let me see it."

You can guess the rest . . . time after time! Many very significant sales later, Peter was smashing his targets, and other salespeople started to emulate him.

So, what's the problem? Answer: A massive peak in customer complaints of overselling followed by consequential discounts, major returns of machines and supplies, and damage to the company reputation.

The third reason that we keep designing processes that are destined to fail is that those in the positions charged with driving up performance don't know what else to do.

Traditional performance management processes have received virtually universal condemnation from those who have seriously analyzed their impact. In the majority of the current fast-paced, highly connected workplaces, the managers' loathing of and the employees' concerns about these processes are well justified.

What Does It Take to Produce an Incentive Scheme That Works?

The intention of this book is not to be a primer for compensation managers, so we will keep this section brief. However, it is important to understand the challenges faced if you are going to rely on incentives. (Generally, we would not rely on incentives, and we explain why later!)

For an incentive scheme to stand a chance of success, the following factors need to be addressed.

THE BUDGET. There needs to be a transparent means of determining the budget to be used. This needs to be based on a clearly observable measure that links directly with the behaviors that you are attempting to drive. It also needs to make commercial sense as well as make sense to those being incentivized. In other words, the potential incentive payments need to be in line with the perceived effort or risk demanded to achieve them.

THE BUDGET ALLOCATION MODEL. The basis on which the budget is to be allocated needs to be clear and in line with the message. For example, if you are claiming to incentivize personal development, then bigger awards should go to the people who developed the most, not necessarily to those who produced the most output or remained highly capable but who are no better off in terms of their professional development than they were at the outset.

THE NATURE OF THE WORK. Evidence has clearly shown that it is possible to incentivize work that is simple, repetitive, or in a managed process. However, when there is a need for even a small level of cognitive ability or problem solving, the power of incentives decreases dramatically.

THE PREDICTABILITY OF THE PAYMENTS. The impact of an incentive is strongly correlated with the ability of those being targeted to predict their likely payment up to a point. There is some evidence that, even then, as they predict achieving what they hoped for, the impact of the incentive subsides (the "I've earned enough this month" syndrome).

THE DEPENDABILITY OF THE PAYMENTS. One of the major factors that dilutes the impact of incentive schemes is *trust*. Employees have to believe that (a) the scheme will be administered with integrity and (b) that there is a good chance that success can be achieved.

One of the major reasons that team incentives fail is that the targets are set on the basis that the relatively weaker team members will up their game, but the top performers do not see this as realistic so, as they expect the team to fail, they drop their own performance.

THE BUDGET HORIZON. Each employee has a budget horizon—the period over which they plan or merely foresee their funds and especially their disposable income. If the incentive is likely to be paid within this time window, it can have a positive impact, but its incentive value declines extremely rapidly if the payment will fall outside that timeline.

THE EMPLOYEES' PERSONAL DISCRETIONARY FUNDS. Most of us have a sense of how much we have spare to spend on nonessentials. For incentives to work, they have to relate to those figures. For people who have a few spare dollars at the end of the month, a serious chance of earning a few hundred extra could make a difference and incentivize them. For people with thousands of spare dollars, a few hundred would "not be worth the effort."

THE PERSONALITIES. There are simply people who are motivated by money and those who are not.

THE VALIDITY OF THE BASE SALARY. If people feel that they are underpaid, you would expect that they would be motivated by the offer of a monetary incentive, but the opposite appears to be the case: if people believe that they are underpaid in terms of their secure base pay, they can easily be demotivated by an incentive that makes them feel that they are being tricked into working hard to get what they believe they already deserve.

THE FAIRNESS OF THE INCENTIVE SCHEME. Despite an apparent uptick in selfish attitudes (a personal peeve of us both), it does appear that the perceived fairness of incentive schemes— even, surprisingly, in the minds of those who are perceived as being favored—is a significant factor in whether they work or not. Consider the following example.

The Head of Compensation for a marketing company was meeting with two research department managers to explain a proposed incentive scheme. She started by explaining the plan. "So the average team of 10 could earn a team pot of up to $13,500. There typically will be one team leader (salary $70,000), five analysts (salary $50,000), one project manager (salary $40,000), two researchers (salary $35,000), and one administrator (salary $20,000). That means that the pot will be around 3 percent of the total salaries. I suggest that we award the team leader 5 percent of the pot and then, in the spirit of teamwork, award the team leader and the team members all the same percentage of their salaries. That will be around 2.8 percent each and the team leader, 3.8 percent."

"I agree, the team leader should be rewarded for her role and everyone else equally."

The other manager was not happy. "But that isn't equal. On my team, Jean, the administrator, will play a major role; the administration on these projects is horrendous. Jean will get only about $570 against the team leader's $2,670. You call that fair? I can tell you now, Jean will tell the team leader and the project manager to do their own administration other than the core stuff. At the moment Jean wet-nurses both of them!"

THE WAY IT'S PAID: RECURRING PAY OR NONRECURRING BONUSES. One of the most significant issues that organizations face now is the result of reckless incentive and reward schemes from early years. Most organizations years ago designed incentive and reward schemes that moved individuals up through the salary bands (that is, they receive recurring rewards) based on a single annual performance, not on proven enhanced capability. So they keep paying repeatedly for the same historical performance.

Why Do People Take Jobs Based on Incentive Schemes?

The following are some of the reasons why people take jobs that have so-called financial incentives:

- They are desperate for money and can't find anything better. They may perform well in the short term, but they are likely to either (a) succeed and move to a better position as soon as they can or (b) become worn down by the stress that such roles inflict.
- They have very short financial horizons: (a) they don't plan or manage their finances well, or (b) they are working to a short-term goal—for example, saving up for a deposit promised to their partner.
- They have limited if any discretionary spending money, and they want to get out of that situation.
- They are just good at these jobs, so typically they get the high rewards.
- They enjoy risk taking.
- They have high levels of self-confidence: "I can do this—I'll show you!"

What Are the Risks for Their Teams?

The following are some of the risks associated with recruiting those types of people into your team:

- They typically don't make dependable team players because they only "show up" when there is financial incentive for them to do so. They are TeamMe players.
- They often give the minimum compliance possible—they comply just with the things that can impact the payment.
- They may make zero attempts to enhance quality unless that is in the incentive measure. (It was the proven dramatic increases in the relatively hidden costs of such working practices that led

to the "quality" movement in the late 1970s and early 1980s. Organizations discovered that "the total cost of quality" often exceeded any perceived value from increased productivity.)

- They will typically collaborate only if it is in their self-interest to do so, otherwise they have no use for their fellow team members or the team leader.
- They burn out.
- They take risks, test boundaries, and cut corners.
- They often suffer from boredom and lack of engagement.
- They produce high error rates unless accuracy is specifically in the incentive measure.
- If quotas are team dependent, interpersonal issues can easily arise and become corrosive. Top performers may actually reduce their efforts.
- There are increased customer (internal and external) complaints, returns, credits, or service failures.

How Should an Organization Devise SuperTeam Incentives?

It is perfectly possible to devise incentives that do work. But they are by far the exception.

If you can address each of the issues above, then you may be able to create a SuperTeam incentive scheme. But be careful, as there is a considerable chance that, if you truly have a SuperTeam, you have individuals who are not going to be motivated primarily by money, in fact, introducing financial incentives may actually create team dysfunction. You may well want to consider a combination of fair rewards and the recognition that super players relish.

Rewards

Rewards are typically the not-at-risk component of an employee's pay. Most organizations seek to bring rigor to determining rewards based on the following factors.

Job Evaluations

Organizations determine the relative worth of each job to the organization based on the demands that it makes of any suitable incumbents.

Pay Bands

Job evaluations nearly always cluster around certain values with gaps between them. Pay bands are typically designed to encompass groups of job sizes or values, although some organizations do assign discrete salaries, rather than salary bands, to specific jobs. Over the past couple of decades, wide pay bands have enabled salary drift, and many organizations are moving back to tighter bands and even spot salaries (that is, fixed salaries for each role with no plus or minus bands around them).

Market Rate Comparisons and Assigning Pay Rates

As part of the process of determining the salary range (or band) for any group of jobs, organizations typically take well-known jobs (or "benchmark" jobs) that also exist in other similar companies and study market rates for those.

To decide the pay rates for each band, this benchmark data is combined with the organization's own performance and its need to attract and keep staff. The resulting pay rate is usually the midpoint of a pay band that is set this way, and that rate is assumed to be the pay that is most appropriate to a fully competent incumbent performing at the expected level—that is, a 100 percent competent individual.

Pay bands typically have a range of ±20 percent.

One of the weaknesses of this approach is that organizations can be held hostage by other employers continuously raising their entry salaries.

Compa-Ratios

Individual employees are slotted into the pay bands based on their perceived competence (unless incentive pay has corrupted this by moving people based on ad hoc performance). This position can be reviewed periodically based on evidence of capability, although most organizations corrupt this measure by including episodic achievements rather than pure capability.

The *compa-ratio* is the measure of how far up the band they are. It is calculated as the employee's current salary divided by the midpoint of the salary band into which his or her job has been placed.

Rewards for SuperTeams

Make sure that you have robust rewards in place—that the true value of each job is fully understood, that you have fair, equitable, and defensible pay in place, and that you have an effective means of ensuring that each individual is appropriately awarded in accordance with those designs.

A reward is payment for past performance. It reaffirms personal worth, builds trust in the organization, and secures commitment to the immediate future (in anticipation of repeat rewards). It rarely produces any sustained increase in motivation, productivity, or efficiency in the future.

Recognition

We have already described the RESPECT Model in which recognition is a key driver. We are not going to go over that again here, other than to state categorically that:

> ## RECOGNITION IS THE MAJOR TRIGGER, ENHANCER, AND SUSTAINER OF INDIVIDUAL MOTIVATION.

On Your Playing Field

Reflecting on Incentives

If you either now have or are thinking about implementing an incentive scheme (which we strongly recommend against doing so unless all of the appropriate conditions are met), here are some questions to consider:

1. Is there a valid and reliable measure that can be used to drive a team incentive for your team—one that can be strongly linked to the team process or behaviors that are to be incentivized?
2. What is it that you need to incentivize about the team? If it is outputs, what processes and behaviors need to change

to achieve them? How can they be measured? Can they be differentiated among the team members?
3. Is the type of work that your team does really suitable for incentives?
4. How could you devise a scheme that would give team members visibility of what they may receive?
5. Do your team members trust the team leader and the organization? Will they believe that the scheme will be implemented without manipulation?
6. Do you have a relatively homogeneous team in terms of the members' financial positions? Are their budget horizons likely to be similar? Are the levels of their discretionary incomes likely to be similar?
7. Is your team made up of people who appear to be really concerned about money—enough so that they will think about it each day and change their behavior to earn more?
8. Do the team members believe that their pay rates are currently appropriate for the work that they do?
9. What do you believe would be the mindset of the team members with respect to the issue of fairness? Would they accept equal percentages or equal absolute amounts, or would they want individual awards—and, if so, how would these awards be determined?
10. How would you want to pay the incentive? Is what you need to be achieved better reflected in a salary increase (that is, demonstrated increase in capability that can be capitalized over and over again) or in a nonrecurring bonus (above the expected episodic target achievement, which might not be achieved again)?

Reflecting on Rewards

1. Is there a robust method for evaluating the relative worth of the jobs in your team? If so, have those evaluations been conducted sufficiently recently?
2. Is there a robust method for grouping jobs in your team? If so, are there market comparisons that can contribute to pay rate setting?

3. Is there a robust method for evaluating individual team members' capabilities and thus positioning them in the pay bands?
4. Do the above formulas work well? If so, are they left to work as they were designed to do, or do other processes corrupt them?

Reflecting on Recognition

1. To what extent do you use recognition as a planned tactic for triggering, reinforcing, sustaining, and enhancing desired performance?
2. What can you do better to recognize individual performance?

Wrap-Up

While performance incentives are intuitively attractive, there is scant evidence of their success and substantial evidence of their doing harm.

Very specific factors must be addressed if incentives are to be effective in a team environment—they are unlikely to help produce a SuperTeam.

Rewards play a key role in laying down a satisfying foundation for team members, ensuring that they feel securely and fairly paid so that they can perform at their best and be open to further encouragement.

Recognition is the biggest driver of sustained team performance—SuperTeams are fueled by it.

SuperTeams not only recognize their individual and collective performances but they also address performance shortfalls promptly, directly, and specifically—they resolve them one way or the other!

Up Next

In the next chapter we explore team diversity and how it can enable a SuperTeam to perform at an even higher level.

CHAPTER 19

Seizing the Benefits of Team Diversity

> Diversity: the art of thinking independently together.
>
> —*Malcolm Forbes*

Overview

International trade and mass migration have expanded rapidly over the past few decades. Most of us find ourselves in very diverse teams or working environments. Yet, those from different nations, races, tribes, and religions still seem to struggle to get along with one another. We also experience other differences, not connected to geography, that divide us, such as gender, age, sexual orientation, and so on. While majorities in all groups say they want to treat one another equally, something just stops it from happening. You could be forgiven for thinking that "people really don't want to get along."

Diversity is not something that a SuperTeam seeks. A SuperTeam seeks to maximize its performance by seizing on the benefits that diversity brings. Diversity is not the end. It is the means!

In this chapter, you will learn:

- The different types of prejudices that people hold and how those prejudices inhibit building diverse teams
- The ways in which diversity can affect team performance
- The ways in which you can benefit from diversity within your team

SUPERSTARTER QUESTIONS

1. How many characteristics (list them) can you identify that differentiate people—for example, race, gender, or age?
2. In what ways are you most different from your other team members? How do or could those differences add value to your team?
3. In what ways are your team members most alike? How might those similarities hinder team performance?
4. What preconceived ideas do you have about each of the groups you have identified—for example, older people typically have a better work ethic; younger people tend to make better use of technology?

TEAM ASSESSMENT

Instructions: Read each statement below, and, using the following scale, decide how accurately it describes your team:

Strongly disagree: 0 points
Disagree: 1 point
Agree: 2 points
Strongly agree: 3 points

Place the point value of your answer choice on the blank line at the beginning of each statement below:

_____ 1. **When looking for a new team member, we pay special attention to finding someone who will** bring new knowledge, skills, values, and thinking to the team.

_____ 2. As a team, we truly value differences in others.

_____ 3. When we have difficult interactions within the team, we explore how these might be arising due to the individual team members coming from diverse backgrounds.

_____ 4. When we have difficult interactions between the team and others outside of it, we explore how these might be arising due to the players coming from diverse backgrounds.

_____ 5. When developing plans and work allocations, we inform those decisions by reviewing the strengths, limitations, and diversity characteristics of each team member.

_____ Total score

INTERPRETING YOUR SCORES

0 to 5: Okay, your team appears to have some pretty strong tribal characteristics. This might be limiting the richness of your discussions, creativity, and relationship building. You are probably recruiting in your own likeness and trying to iron out differences rather than make use of them. It may be a challenge to develop respect within the team or to build it with others outside the team as you are probably all judging one another rather than valuing what one another brings.

6 to 10: Your team seems to recognize that others may think and act differently, but this does not automatically mean that they are bad or poor performers. There is plenty of opportunity to look for and find the value in the differences in others on your team. You probably see opportunities to capitalize on one another's differences, but you may not have gotten around to doing that yet.

11 to 15: Your team appears to have a very good understanding of the value of diversity when the differences are put to good use, and any conflict they may trigger is well managed. You may be a SuperTeam, or you may be close to it.

ASSESSMENT REFLECTION EXERCISE

We cannot avoid categorizing people or even holding perceptions about different groups; to some extent that is human. But we can learn to be aware of our stereotyping, and we can take steps to correct any biases that arise in our decisions because of those stereotypes, many of which are likely to be incorrect.

Various factors trigger us to see others as different and to treat them accordingly. In the past, the primary ones have been religion, class, color, race, nationality, and gender. More recently, education, speech, intelligence (verbal, numeric, and abstract reasoning), personality (using a variety of models as criteria), sexual orientation, age, weight, smoking, physical strength, physical appearance, attire and/or grooming, and personal interests have all been highlighted.

Slowly, more and more factors that influence our perceptions are being identified (and then made illegal as factors that can be allowed to influence our judgments and actions in employment-related decisions).

1. Which of the diversity groups you identified trigger your immediate opinions about other people? (You can be honest with yourself—we are not asking you to share your answers.)
2. Think about yourself. What are the characteristics that you believe define your true self?
3. How different from you are each of your fellow team members?
4. What does your answer to the previous question tell you about the diversity in your team and the differences that you could seek to capitalize on?

Diversity

We all find ourselves in increasingly diverse environments. Many of these situations are in physical meetings, and increasingly, we are also on virtual teams, without the benefits of physical contact. Even modern video connections fail to provide the same visual landscape that physical proximity produces.

We all make instant judgments about those with whom we interact, and it is now thought that those judgments are not made solely on what we see and hear. Research is being done into the senses that are used to collect the information we use and the methods by which our brain processes those data. We each have our own library of stereotypes or groups—models we use to help us create our own picture of what these other (different) people are like. We each react, often subconsciously or instinctively, when we notice that others belong to different groups, "she's/he's black/white, male/female, old/young, pretty/ugly, smart/unkempt, Christian/Muslim, tattooed/ not tattooed, . . ." and differences typically trigger questions or suspicions.

In an attempt to identify or to explain other groups, we label them—for example, "Oh, he's just a youngster" or "He's a Brit—of course he would say that." Such "labeling" is also used by politicians and negotiators as a way of downplaying the other party. It is often used to position the other groups as inferior to us.

If we are to build and sustain a SuperTeam, we need to ensure that all of our judgments (when selecting team members and when working with them) are valid.

In a civilized society, we accept that we are all of equal value and that we do not have to be the same! However, how we each view one another is a complex amalgam of numerous perceptions. Legislation has curbed the excesses of discrimination based on prejudice and stereotyping, and over time, it will enforce habits that may slowly impact our core beliefs. But we have a long way to go before we all truly value and treat one another equally, "because that is how it is." It seems that nature has implanted in us a general tendency to prefer people "like us."

All animals are equal, but some animals are more equal than others.

—*George Orwell,* Animal Farm

But we can train ourselves (a) to be aware of the triggers, assumptions, and prejudices, and (b) to behave in ways that mitigate against any biases they produce in our judgments, decisions, and actions.

Building a Diverse Team

We now look at six issues from the perspective of diversity—making entry to the team easy, engaging new entrants, not being distracted by differences that don't matter, retaining those who are different, being accountable for maintaining diversity, and creating ambassadors.

Make Entry Easy

1. Have you ever found yourself on a team or in a group where you clearly did not fit in? If so, how did it feel?
2. What did you want to do?
3. Have you ever been invited to an event when you've known that you were going to be the odd person out? If so, what did you do?
4. How did you feel?

If your team develops a reputation for being made up of elderly, brilliant, geeky individuals who work long hours, guess what types of people are going to apply for positions on your team!

Have you ever noticed that anybody driving slower than you is an idiot, and anyone going faster than you is a maniac?

—*George Carlin*

Engage Diverse Players

SuperTeams go out of their way to make it clear when they need a specific type of person; they also make it clear that diversity is welcomed around that core requirement. They make it easy for different people to apply, to be selected, and to join—not despite, but because of, their differences.

Empathy is a powerful antidote for prejudice. If we can put ourselves in others' shoes, understand how they feel and why, and understand how that may make them behave, then we can better determine how best to work with them.

America's strength is not our diversity; our strength is our ability to unite people of different backgrounds around common principles. A common language is necessary to reach that goal.

—*Ernest Istook*

Teams do not become stronger merely by becoming diverse—in fact, if not managed well, diversity can have the opposite effect. Teams become stronger when they value and make effective use of the increased capability that diversity offers.

I know there is strength in the differences between us. I know there is comfort, where we overlap.

—*Ani DiFranco*

In the 1990s, the U.S. Marine Corps experienced issues of trust in their leadership. They implemented an initiative to help the leaders identify the differences that their subordinates brought and how to benefit from those. Part of this initiative was the training program "Team Marine." This training introduced a new set of expectations—what belonging to the Marine Corps meant:

1. We expect to actively contribute to the team and to be recognized for our contributions.
2. We expect to be judged fairly and to be recognized and rewarded for our performance.
3. We expect the opportunity to develop our abilities.
4. We expect to be treated professionally and respectfully by other members of our team.
5. We expect to be valued as unique individuals.

In your team, how are the individuals' unique characteristics, capabilities, and interests identified, considered, and made the best use of (rather than being ignored or treated as a reason for sidelining them)?

In the RESPECT Model, the driver always most at risk is *trust*, and trust is most easily damaged by the erroneous perceptions of others. These faulty perceptions can easily arise if we do not actively engage with one another.

SuperTeams actively engage new team members and get to know them well and quickly. They trust them to play a meaningful role early on. They actively seek to learn what new knowledge, skills, and ways of doing things they bring.

Focus on Goals—Don't Be Distracted by Differences

How can you govern a country which has 246 varieties of cheese?

—Charles de Gaulle

Increased awareness of the differences in other people, while intended to enable us to see the equal value in them, can actually have the opposite effect.

For example, one of the challenges that many disabled people face is that others make too many, not too few, allowances for them. As a consequence, they do not get the opportunity to contribute as fully as they are capable.

For example, one of the challenges that wheelchair-bound people face is that speaking from "down there" when others are standing puts them at a disadvantage. This reduced influence could be viewed as resulting from their disability. In fact, however, it arises from the team not seriously engaging the wheelchair-bound people—that is, by the team not showing respect and sitting down too!

Don't Drive Out Diversity

Have you ever seen anyone chased off a team because he did not fit in? Have you ever felt out of place and either left a team or felt that you could not perform at your best on it? When it happens, the arguments are virtually always defensible and logical . . . the reality, however, can be quite different! So the challenge is not merely to build and make effective use of a diverse team. Rather, it is to retain the members of that team. Take note that there is growing evidence that the verbal bullying and marginalizing of individuals that we rightly deplore in schools is perhaps no less prevalent in teams at work!

At bottom every man knows well enough that he is a unique being, only once on this earth; and by no extraordinary chance will such a marvelously picturesque piece of diversity in unity as he is, ever be put together a second time.

—Friedrich Nietzsche

Oftentimes, what makes people leave a team has little if anything to do with the work. It is the unconscious creation of a tribe within the team, and individuals feel as though they are outside of that tribe, in a kind of subset of the team. These are some examples of tribes within teams that we've seen:

- The team developed the habit of socializing on Wednesday nights, not realizing that the one person on the team who couldn't make Wednesdays felt excluded.
- Some members of the team constantly talked about football, knowing that the other team members couldn't stand football.
- The team outsourced statistical analysis even though there was a member of the team who would have loved to do it.
- Some of the team members within the team made jokes in very poor taste about a particular group of other people, not realizing that one of the team members had a close relative in the group being made fun of.
- The team leader consistently gave work of a certain type to the same subset of the team even though there were other team members who were qualified to do that work.

These mini-tribes within a team can have a debilitating effect on other team members and eventually on the team as a whole.

SuperTeams understand that finding great team players is tough; finding great team players who bring diverse knowledge, skills, and attitudes is even harder. So SuperTeams go out of their way to retain their team members and ensure that they play key roles in the team's work.

Be Accountable for Maintaining Diversity

It is often said that "people join companies (or teams) yet leave managers." It could be equally argued that "employees join teams yet leave cliques and prejudice."

A culture of diversity can never flourish if prejudicial behavior is tolerated. SuperTeams ensure that it is not tolerated and that there are clear and strict processes for calling out and addressing any forms of prejudicial behavior.

Make the Team Members the Team's Ambassadors

SuperTeams have pride based on their confidence in what they do and how they do it (their pride is not based on arrogance). All of the team members are therefore the team's ambassadors. They understand and communicate to others:

- The importance of their shared goals.
- The value of teamwork. Seizing on the added capacity and capability of a group of diverse people, combining their knowledge, skills, and efforts to achieve their goals.
- The value of diversity. They bring a blend of complementary knowledge and skills to increase flexibility, adaptability, and overall capability.
- How to seize on the benefits that diversity brings.

The Impact of Culture

Cultural differences have major impacts on how teams, companies, and even countries and nations operate. Consequently, many people have studied the characteristics of national cultures and how these impact human interactions. Most notable of these researchers is Geert Hofstede who, over a period of time between the 1960s and 2010, and supported by others, empirically derived six dimensions that explain how people from different nationalities, on average, behave.

Power Distance Index (PDI)

This dimension describes how power is shared and the extent to which the less powerful accept and/or expect that power to be distributed. It also describes how a society handles inequalities among its members. Within a team, this dimension impacts how the team members view authority and the way in which they expect to be treated.

- Which of your team members appear happy to accept a hierarchical structure with power at the top?
- Which of your team members appear to want everyone to be treated equally, with little hierarchical team structure?

Individualism Versus Collectivism (IDV)

This is the "I" and "we" dimension, and it is especially relevant to teamwork. Individualism describes cultures in which members look after only themselves and those closely related or connected to them. Individuals from these cultures work well with individual targets, personal rewards, and formal one-to-one processes. They argue for others to be held individually accountable.

Collectivism describes cultures that are much more tightly knit. Loyalty is highly valued, and people look out for one another even outside of formal relationships. Individuals from these cultures are supportive of one another, find collective responsibility more appropriate, and want to share rewards.

- Which of your team members appear to want to be treated individually and for others to be held individually accountable too?
- Which of your team members appear to want collective responsibility and want credit and rewards to be shared?

Masculinity Versus Femininity (MAS)

Here we use the terms "masculinity" and "femininity" as technically defined by Geert Hofstede, not as more colloquially or stereotypically used.

So, the masculinity side describes cultures that place a high value on achievement, heroism, assertiveness, competitiveness, and material reward for results. The femininity side describes those with greater appreciation for cooperation, collaboration, modesty, looking after one another, and the quality of life.

- Which of your team members appear to be most interested in the outputs of the team, taking control, getting stuff done, and expecting a bonus for doing it?
- Which of your team members appear to be more interested in how they can work better together and share any benefits that accrue from their work?

Uncertainty Avoidance Index (UAI)

This dimension describes how uncertainty and ambiguity are handled.

- Which of your team members appear to thrive on uncertainty and ambiguity? Do they actively work with these issues and find creative solutions when needed?
- Which of your team members do not appear to cope well with uncertainty and ambiguity? Do they become paralyzed and find it difficult to make decisions?

Long-Term Versus Short-Term Orientation (LTO)

This dimension describes individuals' natural time horizons. Are they focused on the here and now? Do they argue that "in the long term, there is no long term"?

- Which of your team members typically want to focus on the short-term, tactical issues?
- Which of your team members are always demanding to know what the long-term strategy is?

Indulgence Versus Restraint (IVR)

We love this one! Indulgence describes cultures in which enjoying life and having fun are highly valued. Restraint describes cultures that apply stricter social norms.

- Is your team one in which most team members believe that people having fun do better work? If so, which team members disagree?
- How does their attitude affect the way they participate?
- How does their attitude affect the rest of the team?
- Is your team one in which most team members believe that the work they do demands a more restrained and serious approach? If so, which team members agree? If so, which team members disagree?
- How does their attitude affect the way they participate?
- How does their attitude affect the rest of the team?

The Importance of Language

I know you think you understand what you thought I said, but I'm not sure you realize that what you heard is not what I meant.

—*Alan Greenspan*

Language is the primary tool of teamwork. Without communications, virtually nothing can be achieved collectively. Yet, this is a key, if not the primary, differentiating characteristic of human beings. How often have you been in a meeting in which people were speaking in a different language and they knew that you could not understand them? Doesn't it drive you nuts? Of course, they always argue, "It helped us to be more precise," or "Sorry, we didn't realize." Probably true, and it still drives me nuts!

If you want a SuperTeam, make sure that language differences are handled respectfully. Respect your fellow team members; acknowledge native language differences; use languages that you can all understand; and whenever practical (even if having to use translators), use their language. If team members are going to use a nonshared language for a specific and valid reason, get them to explain their comments in the group's usual language or get them to find time to have their conversation outside the meeting, when others will not be left waiting unnecessarily. Understand that languages have different constructs and even ranges of vocabulary. For example, "You should do X" in one language may translate best into "Why don't you consider this as an idea" while in another it is interpreted as an unequivocal command. We have to make allowances, and check our understanding . . . before reacting!

Here's another peeve of ours. Acronyms and codes are taking over the world!

If you want to be a SuperTeam, ensure that your team communicates in ways that bring clarity, preciseness, and understanding. Stamp out as many acronyms and other coded language terms that are potentially divisive. They separate us into those "who know and understand" and "those who don't"—use of acronyms and codes can easily create a diversity dimension that does not need to separate us!

And here's another peeve. Good use of language (spelling and grammar) is a reasonable expectation, especially in business. But don't judge others merely on their accent, diction, pronunciation, or even style. Stereotyping based on language can lead to serious errors in our judgment of people. Also, be aware that those from other countries may actually speak your language more correctly than you do—foreign-language teachers rarely teach the colloquial language. Those from other countries may well find fault with you!

Do your team members communicate respectfully with one another? Do they wait for one another to finish before speaking? Do they acknowledge one another? Do they build on one another's ideas rather than attacking or undermining them? Do they show common courtesies? Do they speak with and to one another rather than about one another?

In a SuperTeam, team members actively listen and seek to understand one another's perspectives. One of the most important communication skills is paraphrasing—for example, "Let me be sure I understand what you are saying." Such a statement not only ensures that you have accurately heard your team member, but it also demonstrates respect by showing that you are actively listening and care about what she has to say.

The Importance of Location

Teams that are diverse by location, including virtual teams, face a number of specific challenges, not the least of which are the following:

1. Scheduling (getting hold of people to agree on dates and times). Show *consideration*, and ask the various team members what works best in terms of notice, start times, duration, days of the week or month, and so on. Make expectations of team members clear in terms of what needs to happen ahead of the meetings—for example, submission of information that can be made accessible to others, during the meetings—for example, meeting etiquette, and after the meetings—for example, following through on commitments.

SuperTeams take special care to ensure that all team members are treated fairly and that their preferences are taken into account when meetings are scheduled.

2. Connections (telephone, VOIP, audio or video). Show *consideration*, and ask the various team members what works best for them. What equipment do they have access to? Will they incur fees if they use one over the other? Are the meetings going to be in a private or a public location?

SuperTeams focus on ensuring that everyone has the best possible connection to see and hear without adverse interruption or cost.

3. Information sharing. Work out how best to share information such as agendas, minutes, presentations, and submissions. Will you use cloud or intranet services? Will you e-mail? Will you simply screen share during the meeting? Your choices may vary depending on the type of meeting and the topics to be discussed. In some cases, you may need to incur shipping costs—for example, you may need to discuss a product, and each person's needs to have one in his or her hands.

SuperTeams have highly efficient means of sharing information, especially those documents that need to be edited remotely.

4. Chairing. Typically the team leader chairs meetings, but this does not have to be the case. Chairing a meeting is an opportunity to *empower* a team member to learn the skill. It is also an opportunity to allow an expert on the team to take the chair for highly detailed discussions. In the case of a virtual meeting, anyone could chair, and SuperTeams make use of that flexibility, largely for development reasons.

5. Attendance. Virtual meetings suffer from the same challenges as colocated meetings: how do you get team members to attend, and how do you get team members to arrive on time? There is also the added complication of engaging non-team members on an ad hoc basis.

Most teams make use of virtual meeting technology, and this typically comes with scheduling tools that post the meetings to the team members' calendars. They also include automated e-mail or text reminders that can be sent to desktop computers and smartphones.

SuperTeams agree on meeting etiquette, which includes attending, arriving on time, and ensuring that the meetings start and end on time.

6. Collaboration during meetings. We are all aware of the various forms of participation at face-to-face meetings. Some people take up significant airspace, some say nothing, some get assertive, and some get angry.

In a virtual meeting, it is much harder to (a) monitor how others in the meeting are feeling (even when using web technology because this often focuses only on the speaker), (b) know if team members are really *attending* the meeting or if they are present but doing other things at their end, and (c) interject and do something about these participation issues.

Advances in technology are, however, now making videoconferencing over the Internet practical (with a highlighted image of the person who is speaking). Collaborative whiteboards, virtual brain maps, virtual breakout rooms, and borderless presentation media are now available and creating very realistic virtual meeting rooms.

SuperTeams are not always the early adopters, but they do continuously look at the tools that are available and explore their potential return on investment for the team.

Virtual teams are now a feature of everyday life in even the smallest of organizations. The goal is to utilize the tools that are now available and to ensure that everyone:

- *Recognizes* the valuable contributions by others.
- Is *empowered* to participate virtually if appropriate.
- Provides *supportive feedback* to others to acknowledge that they are there and contributing.

- Identifies opportunities to better *partner*.
- Knows the *expectations* in terms of attendance, preparation, participation, and follow-through.
- Shows *consideration* for the other team members who may be in quite different circumstances
- *Trusts* one another until that trust is proven false.

On Your Playing Field

1. Which stereotypes do you think most affect your judgment of others? Find some people who superficially fit that stereotype, and get to know them better—you may be surprised!
2. Think about your team. How is it composed? Would people from more diverse backgrounds feel at ease applying to join? What can you do to make it more obvious to those outside the team that you welcome diversity?
3. Think about your team. How are the team members engaged? Has stereotyping potentially affected role assignment? Could team members have richer roles? Could team members add more value by using knowledge and skills that are currently underemployed?
4. Think about your team. Who is at risk of leaving (for whatever reason)? Will their leaving weaken the diversity of the team? If so, how might you encourage or enable them to stay?
5. Think about your team. Who are your real ambassadors who promote the team and its diversity? If you have none, whom might you encourage to take on this important role?
6. Read up on the issue of national cultures, and identify how this may be impacting the way in which your team members interact. Do their national cultures explain why some interactions work well? Do they explain why some interactions do not work well?
7. Think about your team. Consider the issue of language. Do team members use language constructively with one another? Are communications clear, concise, and accurate? Are common courtesies articulated? Do team members take responsibility for their own understanding and check it if in doubt?

8. If you have virtual team meetings, are you thinking about the needs of those who are in positions that are different from yours in terms of time, equipment, culture, and so on? How could you change the way the team works to make your virtual meetings more effective?

Wrap-Up

It is not diversity alone that makes a SuperTeam. A SuperTeam capitalizes on its diversity—it makes use of the different knowledge, skills, and ways of thinking and doing things.

SuperTeams:

- Ensure that it is easy for those from diverse backgrounds to apply and join the team.
- Proactively engage members from diverse backgrounds.
- Focus on the team's goals—they are not distracted by minor diversity issues. They work through any disconnects.
- Actively retain great talent including those who bring diversity to the team.
- Address possible communication barriers.
- Understand that we each come with certain beliefs and values and that these contribute to our national cultures. SuperTeams understand those differences, take them into account, and work to seize on the benefits that they can bring.
- Understand the different dynamics that virtual meetings create and do not assume that these are resolved merely by the use of technology.

Up Next

Now that you are equipped to create a new SuperTeam, to evolve your current team into a SuperTeam, or to celebrate already being in a SuperTeam, please contact us—Paul@PaulMarciano.com and Clinton@ClintonWingrove.com—and share your experiences. Also please visit our website—www.SuperTeamsTheBook.com—where you can find additional materials to bring RESPECT alive in your team.

Epilogue

We cannot live only for ourselves. A thousand fibers
connect us with our fellow men; and among those
fibers, as sympathetic threads, our actions run as
causes, and they come back to us as effects.

—Herman Melville

For fun, type "team" into a Google search box, and you'll get over a trillion hits—more than you get for the word "god." If you're looking to read another book on the subject, type the word "team" into an Amazon.com search box, and up pops over 100,000 titles. As a species, we've been living and working in teams for about 200,000 years, and as individuals, we've been involved with teams most of our lives. Given all humankind's experience and accumulated knowledge on the subject, you'd think that we'd be pretty good at teaming by now. Unfortunately, not only do most teams fail to reach their potential, but they are also typically highly dysfunctional.

Don't get us wrong—we know a lot about what goes into the recipe for making a highly effective team. We know that groups of people work best when they have clear and shared goals; singular leadership; a defined team structure with clear team roles; agreed-upon team processes and rules; and quality communications. Many teams, however, can check off all these boxes but still fail to produce better than average results—they certainly aren't SuperTeams. Our research indicates a simple problem that appears difficult to solve:

team dysfunction is caused by the inability or unwillingness of team members to work together with RESPECT: recognition, empowerment, supportive feedback, partnering, expectations, consideration, and trust.

Although beyond the scope of this book, we feel compelled to at least mention the powerful and ubiquitous role of technology in relation to respect and teams. Does technology increase team functioning and promote respect? In most cases, no. Can technology facilitate teamwork? Absolutely. Electronic communications such as internal company blogs, instant messaging, LinkedIn, Skype, FaceTime, e-mail, and texting provide us with lots of tools and platforms that help us connect quickly with others. You can get replies from team members instantly. At the same time, these technologies can detract from team functioning by reducing the time people spend in actual physical interaction.

Both gaining and giving respect are greatly facilitated when we work together physically. There is something very fundamental about "looking someone in the eye" and shaking that person's hand. We need to check one another out. Although some communication is always better than none, whether our team members are on the other side of the wall or on the other side of the world, it must be kept in mind that using technology to communicate diminishes interpersonal contact. From an evolutionary perspective, teamwork began on the ground, not in the cloud.

Technology is fundamentally changing our entire concept of teamwork. Teams can now be composed of transitory connections across time and space, between people who may or may not know each other, and who may or may not connect again. We call such spontaneous and ephemeral teams *connectives*, and we believe they will become the dominant form of collaboration. Who would have thought that a group of people would come together and create a free resource like *Wikipedia*? Or that companies could get start-up funding through crowdsourcing? Or that posting a request on a social media website could help you find the name of your new book? That's where we got the name for *SuperTeams*—no kidding.

When it comes to virtual teams and connectives, you might think that respect does not matter. It does. When people come together virtually to solve problems quickly, interpersonal respect often doesn't matter; however, technical expertise matters a lot. In fact, people build up online reputations based on their expertise, and the more highly respected they are, the more influential they are. If we're collaborating online and you don't know what you're talking about, you could be the greatest guy on earth, but I'd have no interest in putting you on my team.

Obviously, virtual teams are here to stay and will continue to flourish—at least in number. But both social and professional organizations will also continue to rely heavily on traditional teams through which groups of people will work together in close physical proximity over a period of time to accomplish specific tasks, albeit facilitated by technology. However constituted, at the end of the day, teams are composed of people and can be effective only when every member of the group is committed to the other members and to the work they all do together. The only way for them to get there is through fostering mutual respect. What can you do to spread RESPECT in your organization today and move your team closer to being a SuperTeam?

Appendix A

42 SuperTips for Earning Respect from Your Team Members

1. Show others respect.
2. Do your job, and do it well.
3. Offer to lend a hand.
4. Help people out when it is clear they need it.
5. Take the initiative to go above and beyond for the benefit of the team.
6. Act professionally no matter what.
7. Be positive and upbeat.
8. Let people know that you appreciate their work.
9. Do what you say you're going to do. Keep your commitments.
10. Accept responsibility when you screw up.
11. Actively listen to others, and seek to understand their concerns, ideas, and perspectives.
12. Show that you care about your team members by asking them appropriate questions about their life outside of work and what matters to them.
13. Show your commitment to the goals of the team, not your own agenda.
14. Always speak the truth, and be straight with team members—especially if you don't think they want to hear it. Obviously, be tactful and considerate.
15. Demonstrate empathy and compassion.
16. Cover for team members whenever possible.
17. Publicly acknowledge and thank others for their good work or help.
18. Remain calm when things don't go well, and don't point fingers.

19. If possible and appropriate, take a bullet for a team member. Direct any fallout from a problem to you.
20. Take the initiative to become more educated and, thus, a bigger asset to your team.
21. Always speak positively of others.
22. Respond quickly to your team members.
23. Don't complain about circumstances—just do your job the best you can.
24. Stand up for a team member who may be getting mistreated by the team leader, another team member, or a customer.
25. Ask others for their suggestions and advice—and then act on it.
26. Request feedback, especially from more junior team members, on your work, and thank them for giving it to you.
27. Take the initiative to resolve a conflict with another team member.
28. Come to meetings fully prepared.
29. Always be on time.
30. Be a mentor and coach to new or less experienced team members.
31. Give others straight feedback in a supportive and constructive manner.
32. Act with integrity at all times—even when it goes against your personal best interests.
33. Stand up for what you believe is right—especially in the face of opposition.
34. Persevere when the going gets tough.
35. When people make mistakes, be supportive, and try to help them learn from them.
36. Refuse to engage in gossip or office politics.
37. Give credit when credit is due.
38. If you don't know the answer to something, admit that you don't. Don't ever try to fake it.
39. Make sacrifices for the sake of the team—for example, give up some of your resources so another team member can accomplish his or her goals.
40. Be willing to compromise.
41. Let others know that you trust and respect them.
42. Always be humble when it comes to your accomplishments.

Appendix B

Vision

To color the world brighter for all children.

Mission

To create products that foster children's creativity and promote the time-honored values of charitable giving, good manners, and patriotism. Founded on the principle that "giving is good," our company aspires to become a role model for all companies by donating 10 percent of our gross proceeds to children's charities and demonstrating that "giving" makes good business sense.

Guiding Philosophical Principles

1. We seek to make a difference in the lives of children
2. We are a compassionate, kind and giving organization
3. We act honestly, fairly and forthright in all dealings
4. We stimulate creativity and imagination in children
5. We foster traditional, time-honored family values
6. We are a flexible, progressive, "outside of the lines" company
7. We are in a continual process of learning and improving
8. We are a client-centric company that listens to our customers
9. We recognize our team members as our greatest asset
10. We are truly blessed to have these opportunities

ColorMe Company Team Rules

Team Member Expectations

1. Remain committed to and seek to foster ColorMe Company's Mission
2. Act in accordance with our Guiding Philosophical Principles
3. Always represent ColorMe Company with the highest degree of professionalism
4. Use best judgment and good old-fashion common sense at all times
5. Treat our customers as you would want to be treated

Our Team Values . . .

1. Family, and believes that their needs supercede "work" related needs
2. Open communication—especially listening—and the sharing of information and ideas
3. Flexibility, adaptability, and open-mindedness
4. Creativity, independent thinking, initiative, learning, and hard work
5. Individual differences, backgrounds, experiences, beliefs, and dreams

Our Team Believes In . . .

1. Hiring "good" people and providing them with opportunities to learn and grow
2. Teamwork and in helping one another
3. Having fun and enjoying what we do
4. Learning from our experiences; not in making *mistakes*
5. Each other and that together we can make a difference

About the Authors

Dr. Paul Marciano

Paul Marciano is the leading authority on employee engagement and respect in the workplace, and he is the author of the internationally acclaimed book *Carrots and Sticks Don't Work* (McGraw Hill, 2010) and creator of the RESPECT™ Model. Paul earned his doctorate in clinical psychology from Yale University, and he has worked in the field of human resources for more than 25 years. You are invited to visit his website at www.PaulMarciano.com and contact him directly at Paul@PaulMarciano.com.

Clinton Wingrove, DMS, MCIPD

Clinton Wingrove's career started in work measurement and design; it evolved through automation of warehousing, logistics, and HR processes; and he is now an authority and speaker on maximizing performance and development. He believes in the power of technology to enable optimal teamwork and behavior engineering, but he also knows that true discretionary performance is seen only if respect prevails. You may contact him via e-mail at clinton@clintonwingrove.com or visit his website at www.clintonwingrove.com.

Employee recognition programs don't work.
All you need is a little
R.E.S.P.E.C.T.

Learn Dr. Paul Marciano's proven employee-engagement model.

"This book should be in the hands of anyone who has to get work done through other people!"
—John L. Rice, Vice President Human Resources, Tyco International

0071714014 • $24.95

Notes

Notes

Notes

Notes

Notes

Notes

Notes